Praise for Thomas Chatteron Williams's
Losing My Cool

"*Losing My Cool* is a provocative, intellectual memoir." —*USA Today*

"Invincibly important . . . a startling memior of growing up in the black middle class. . . . What makes it so shocking is its devastating critique of hip hop 'culture' . . . in gripping, comic, and disturbing detail."
—Stanely Crouch, *New York Daily News*

"First-time author Williams offers a revealing memoir on a par with James McBride's *The Color of Water*." —*Library Journal*

"Williams's debut memoir, *Losing My Cool*, boldly and courageously introduces into American public discourse a seldom-discussed ugly truth: Young African Americans are becoming ignorant by choice. Williams's book is desperately needed." —*San Francisco Chronicle*

"It would be a shame if Williams's thoughtful comments about hip-hop, which deserve and undoubtedly will receive articulate response, detract attention from other equally engaging portions of *Losing My Cool*. For example, his portrait of his dad, an intensely private man, contains some of the most compelling writing about black fathers in recent literature on the subject. There is much to admire in *Losing My Cool*, and more to anticipate from Williams." —*The Washington Post Book World*

"This is more than a coming-of-age story; it is an awakening, as Williams blends Dostoyevsky and Jay-Z in a compelling memoir and analysis of urban youth culture." —*Booklist* (starred review)

"*Losing My Cool* is an engaging and honest exploration of one man's self-discovery, as well as the powerful relationship between a father and son." —*The Daily Beast*

"A sobering deconstruction of the harmful hip-hop mindset by a brother who very easily could've ended up a casualty of that dead-end path instead of a role model." —Kam Williams, Baret News Service

"A lot of fun, very very accessible, an[d] Tupac and the Brothers Karamazov in
—Patrik H[

PENGUIN BOOKS

LOSING MY COOL

Thomas Chatterton Williams has written for *The Washington Post*, *The Wall Street Journal*, *The American Scholar*, *The Root*, and *n+1*. He lives in Brooklyn, New York.

LOSING MY COOL

Love, Literature, and a Black Man's
Escape from the Crowd

THOMAS CHATTERTON WILLIAMS

PENGUIN BOOKS

PENGUIN BOOKS

Published by the Penguin Group

Penguin Group (USA) Inc., 375 Hudson Street, New York, New York 10014, U.S.A. • Penguin Group
(Canada), 90 Eglinton Avenue East, Suite 700, Toronto, Ontario, Canada M4P 2Y3
(a division of Pearson Penguin Canada Inc.) • Penguin Books Ltd,
80 Strand, London WC2R 0RL, England • Penguin Ireland, 25 St Stephen's Green,
Dublin 2, Ireland (a division of Penguin Books Ltd) • Penguin Books Australia Ltd,
250 Camberwell Road, Camberwell, Victoria 3124, Australia (a division of Pearson Australia Group Pty Ltd) •
Penguin Books India Pvt Ltd, 11 Community Centre, Panchsheel Park,
New Delhi – 110 017, India • Penguin Group (NZ), 67 Apollo Drive, Rosedale, North Shore
0632, New Zealand (a division of Pearson New Zealand Ltd) • Penguin Books (South Africa)
(Pty) Ltd, 24 Sturdee Avenue, Rosebank, Johannesburg 2196, South Africa

Penguin Books Ltd, Registered Offices: 80 Strand, London WC2R 0RL, England

First published in the United States of America by The Penguin Press,
a member of Penguin Group (USA) Inc. 2010
Published in Penguin Books 2011

1 3 5 7 9 10 8 6 4 2

Grateful acknowledgment is made for permission to reprint excerpts from the following copyrighted works:
No Name in the Street by James Baldwin (Dial Press, 1972). By permission of the James Baldwin Estate.
"The Part About Amalfitano" from *2666* by Roberto Bolaño, translated by Natasha Wimmer. Copyright © 2004
by the heirs of Roberto Bolaño. Translation copyright © 2008 by Natasha Wimmer. Reprinted by permission
of Farrar, Straus and Giroux LLC and The Wylie Agency LLC.

THE LIBRARY OF CONGRESS HAS CATALOGED THE HARDCOVER EDITION AS FOLLOWS:
Williams, Thomas Chatterton, 1981–
Losing my cool : growing up with and out of hip-hop culture / Thomas Chatterton Williams.
p. cm.
ISBN 978-1-59420-263-6 (hc.)
ISBN 978-0-14-311962-3 (pbk.)
1. African Americans—Social conditions.   2. African American youth—Attitudes.
3. African Americans in popular culture.   4. African Americans—Race identity.
5. Popular culture—United States.   6. Hip-hop—United States.   I. Title.
E185.615.W497 2010
305.235'108996073—dc22   2009053251

Printed in the United States of America
DESIGNED BY AMANDA DEWEY

*Penguin is committed to publishing works of quality and integrity.
In that spirit, we are proud to offer this book to our readers;
however, the story, the experiences, and the words
are the author's alone.*

For my parents, Kathleen and Clarence Leon Williams,
and for my brother, Clarence Leon Williams II,
With all my love

"People who cling to their illusions find it difficult, if not impossible, to learn anything worth learning: a people under the necessity
of creating themselves must examine everything, and soak up learning the way the roots of a tree soak up water."

—JAMES BALDWIN

"I understand you . . . I mean, if I'm right, I think I understand you.
You're like me and I'm like you. We aren't happy. The atmosphere
around us is stifling. We pretend there's nothing wrong, but there
is. What's wrong? We're being fucking stifled."

—ROBERTO BOLAÑO

CONTENTS

Preface   *xiii*

CHAPTER ONE

The Discovery of What It Means to Be a Black Boy   *1*

CHAPTER TWO

A Wicked Genie   *19*

CHAPTER THREE

What About Your Friends?   *37*

CHAPTER FOUR

Street Dreams (Who Am I to Disagree?)   *63*

CHAPTER FIVE

Slip the Yoke   *81*

CHAPTER SIX

You Can't Go Home Again *109*

CHAPTER SEVEN

Beginning to See the Light *137*

CHAPTER EIGHT

To a Worm in a Horseradish, the World Is a Horseradish *159*

CHAPTER NINE

Every Secret Loses Its Force *187*

Epilogue *207*

PREFACE

This book was conceived while I was still a student in graduate school. It was initially intended to be an explicit argument, a work of cultural criticism and not a document of my—or, for that matter, anyone else's—personal life. As I began writing, however, my abstract critiques gradually gave way to some very specific anecdotes, and my father's calming voice, along with the rambunctious voices of my neighbors, classmates, and old friends flooded my mind and seeped out onto the page, seemingly with a force all their own. Czeslaw Milosz, the Polish poet, once observed, "When a writer is born into a family, that family is doomed." I know what he means by that. Ultimately, the autobiographical nature of this book has led me to include scenes, stories, descriptions, depictions, quotes, and implications about myself and others with which I am certain my family—especially my father, a very private man— will not be completely at ease seeing in print. The logical question, then, the question I have wrestled with over the past two years, is this: If you know in advance that you are going to disturb the people you love most by writing what you intend to write, why write it at all? The only way one could ever justify doing such a thing, I am convinced, is if the personal information being exposed and dealt with is not splattered about gratuitously but is put to use always in service of some larger idea, some greater good. Mere exhibitionism for its own sake is indefensible at best. It is my sincerest hope, then, that I have met my own standard in the pages that follow and that my love is evident throughout.

An additional concern presented itself as the writing grew more personal. None of the characters who populate this book—classmates, neighbors, friends and enemies alike—was aware at the time of our acquaintance that they were opening themselves up to the scrutiny of a memoirist. With that in mind, and with the exception of my family, certain friends and public figures, the names and identifying characteristics of most of the persons included in this memoir have been changed to protect their privacy.

CHAPTER ONE

The Discovery of What It Means to Be a Black Boy

It was wintertime, early in the morning. I was in the third grade, standing on the rectangular asphalt playground behind Holy Trinity Interparochial School in Westfield, New Jersey, palming a tennis ball, waiting. Ned, nearsighted and infamous for licking the dusty soles of his penny loafers in the back of social studies class, was splayed against the cold orange brick wall of the school building. He had his head down and hands up, legs akimbo with his butt out, like a South American mule bracing herself to be searched by border patrol. "Not so hard!" he cried, glancing back over his shoulder through smudged Coke-bottle lenses.

"Put your head down!" another boy yelled.

"Fine, just do it and get it over with, then," Ned muttered.

"Head down!" the boy said. I wound my arm back and let fly a fastball that seemed to hang in the air for a second before ricocheting from the small of Ned's back like a Pete Sampras ace off some hapless ball boy at Wimbledon. Ned jerked upright and howled in pain. All my classmates screamed and high-fived me as the bell rang and we rushed to grab our book bags and line up in size order before our teachers came to lead us indoors. I was still the undisputed king of Butts-Up, I thought to myself as I pulled my Chicago Bulls Starter jacket over my uniform. Standing in line, waiting for the younger grades to file past, I began mumbling to myself bits of a song by Public Enemy, a song that my older brother had been playing at home and that had gotten stuck in my head that week like the times tables or the Holy Rosary. *"Yo, nigga, yoooooo, nigga, yoooo-oooooo, niiiigga ..."* I repeated the refrain over and over under my breath, unthinkingly, as I relived in my mind's eye the glorious coup de grace, the deathblow I'd just dealt Ned from over ten yards away—*Blaow!*

"But you're a nigger, too," a voice said from behind me, and I half made out what I'd just heard, but not fully. I went on singing my song, which I couldn't claim to understand on any level, but which somehow made me feel cool as hell, and that was all that mattered. The voice repeated itself, louder this time: "But you're a nigger, too, Thomas, aren't you?"

"Huh?" I said, pivoting to see Craig standing there, his dirty-blond hair cut by his mother's Flowbee into the shape of an upside-down serving bowl, like a medieval friar without the bald spot. "What did you just say?"

"You're a nigger, too, right, so how can you say that?"

"How can I say what?"

"'Yo, nigga, yo, nigga'; how can you say that when you're a nigger, too, right?"

———————

My mother is white, my father black. They met in San Diego in the late 1960s. Both were entrenched on the West Coast front of what at the time was called the War on Poverty. After San Diego, they went up to Los Angeles. From L.A. they made their way north and my father pursued doctoral studies in sociology at the University of Oregon. In 1975, and over my maternal grandfather's dead body, they were married in Eugene at the county courthouse. They had little money, fewer blessings, and plenty of love. Later, they moved again to Spokane and my mother, Kathleen, gave birth to their first child, Clarence, named for my father. From Spokane the family continually moved east: first to Denver, then to Albany, then to Philadelphia, and finally to New Jersey, where I was born in 1981.

When I was one year old, my father switched professions and the family moved again, this time from Newark, where he had been running antipoverty programs for the Episcopal Archdiocese and my mother had been raising my brother and me, to Fanwood, a small suburb thirty minutes to the west on U.S. Route 22. Fanwood, like the space inside a horseshoe, is bordered on three sides by the much larger township of Scotch Plains, and these two municipalities by and large function as one. They share a train station and public school system and together act as a kind of buffer ground between wealthy Westfield to the east and poor Plainfield to the west. Riots and waves of white flight long ago left Plainfield a vexed cross between a legitimate inner-city ghetto—with all the requisite crime, poverty, and hopelessness that go with that—and an emergent middle-class suburb that in many ways resembles Westfield, except for the condition of the houses and the color of the residents. No such white flight occurred in Fanwood, Scotch Plains, or Westfield, although like so many small towns in New Jersey, they had their designated black pockets.

When my parents first began searching in the area, real estate brokers only wanted to show them homes in Plainfield or on the redlined black sides of town. They said families like ours tended to prefer things this way, but my father, whom we call Pappy in a nod to his Southern roots, had led a childhood that was boxed in by formal segregation in Texas, and no longer could stand to be told where to live. Out of principle he said to the brokers thank you but no thank you, and insisted on seeing all listings. Reluctantly, they caved and the four of us settled into a three-bedroom ranch on Fanwood's decidedly white side.

It was a neighborhood of well-kept homes with yards that were flaired-up with inflatable IT'S A BOY! lawn signs, lighted holiday displays, and the occasional life-size Virgin Mary shrine. There were two main downtown areas in either direction of our house, with more pizzerias than banks or dry cleaners and, to Pappy's lament, without a single bookstore between them. Our neighbors were what my parents called "ethnic whites," and they tended to grow up, buy homes, have children, and die within a twenty-mile radius of where they had been born—a fact that always seemed to strike Mom and Pappy as bizarre. As a family, we did not fit in with these people, who often didn't know what to make of us. Once when I was a very young boy, I was at the grocery store with my mother, misbehaving as little children do, when an older white woman walked by and said, "Ugh, it must be so tough adopting those kids from the ghetto."

Despite my mother's being white, we were a black and not an

interracial family. Both of my parents stressed this distinction and the result was that, growing up, race was not so complicated an issue in our household. My brother and I were black, period. My parents adhered to a strict and unified philosophy of race, the contents of which boil down to the following: There is no such thing as being half-white, for black, they explained, is less a biological category than a social one. It is a condition of the mind that is loosely linked to certain physical features, but more than anything it is a culture, a challenge, and a discipline. We were taught from the moment we could understand spoken words that we would be treated by whites as though we were black whether we liked it or not, and so we needed to know how to move in the world as black men. And that was that.

Questions of the soul were less clear. My mother is Protestant, the daughter of an evangelical Baptist minister. My father is what he calls a Geopolitical-Existentialist-Secularist-Humanist-Realist, which really is just his way of saying he doesn't put much stock in organized religion. Nevertheless, after very nearly being home-schooled, Clarence and I were enrolled in private Catholic schools for what my father described as "the superior levels of discipline" they offered in relation to the public schools nearby.

Another factor in the decision was the day Clarence came home from School One, about a half-block away from our front door, dazed and unable to speak. He was in the second grade and my father had given him an oxblood leather briefcase. Apparently, this made him stand out among the other boys. So did his sun-tanned skin, which after the long hot summer was the color of maple honey; and his hair, which was styled in a large spherical Afro and which in his childhood was light brown with strands of blond and something like sherry in it: beautiful. My mother and sometimes my father would comb my brother's Afro in the mornings with an orange tin can of Murray's dressing grease and a black plastic pick. "You look distinguished now, son," Pappy would say, and smile when he was finished with him, *distinguished* being the rarest and highest compliment in his vocabulary.

Clarence was a quiet boy with thick hair, good muscle tone, and intelligent almond-shaped eyes beneath bushy brown eyebrows. That day at school a group of white children had cornered and taunted him on the yard, asking what a fucking monkey had to do with a briefcase. Either the other black students didn't see this happen or they chose not to intervene. Pappy yanked Clarence from public school the next day. By the time I was old enough, being in class with our neighbors was not even an option.

Unlike some children of mixed-race heritage, I didn't ever wish to be white. I wanted to be black. One of the first adult books my parents gave to me, around age seven, was Alex Haley's *The Autobiography of Malcolm X*. Often my mother would come into my room in the evening and discuss with me what I was reading. For several nights, I lay awake long after she had turned out the lights, haunted by the image of Malcolm's father lying prone on the railroad tracks, his body torn in two and his cranium cracked open like a coconut husk. I didn't want to resemble in any way whatsoever those men who did things like that to other men.

It was a fortunate thing for me, too, that I didn't want to be white. It was fortunate because I really didn't have much choice in the matter. My parents were right: Around white kids, I simply was not white. Whatever fantasies of passing may have threatened to steal into my mulatto psyche and wreak havoc there were dispelled early on, when Tina turned around in her chair, flipped her bronze ponytail to the side, and asked me point-blank, and audibly enough for the whole classroom to hear, "Hey, why doesn't your hair move like everyone else's?"

"It's because I'm black," I told her, and I wasn't angry or embarrassed. It was just a fact, I felt, the way that she was husky or big-boned.

Though we didn't speak about it outright, I don't think my brother, Clarence, ever wanted to be white, either. He just didn't seem to see race everywhere around him like my parents and I did. Or if he saw it, he fled from it and didn't want to analyze it or have to spend his time unraveling it. He didn't want to be forced to make a big deal out of it. He was forgiving and trusting and found companions wherever they would be his. His two best friends were black, and he dated a quiet Asian girl for a spell during high school. Mostly, though, he fell in with a set of neighborhood white boys with lots of vowels in their surnames and little in their heads. These white boys were almost certainly the same ones who, years earlier, had demeaned my brother with racial epithets on that School One playground (the neighborhood is not that big). But Clarence never knew how to hold a grudge, and that was ages ago and these were his neighbors and they liked to do the things that he liked to do: ride bikes, ride skateboards, talk cars, smoke cigarettes, cut class, hang out. And they did take him in as one of their own, that's true, although I could see even as a child that they did so without ever fully allowing him to rest his mind, to forget that he was black and that he was somehow *other*. Still, I can't fault my brother for going the way he felt was most comfortable. He was a child of the late '70s and '80s; hip-hop hadn't completely circumscribed the world he was formed in. I was a child of the late '80s and '90s, on the other hand. I went the other route.

Not that it was always an easy route to go. It was not enough simply to know and to accept that you were black—you had to look and act that way, too. You were going to be judged by how convincingly you could pull off the pose. One day when I was around nine years old, my mother drove Clarence and me over to Unisex Hair Creationz, a black barbershop in a working-class section of Plainfield. Back then we had a metallic blue, used Mercedes-Benz sedan, which from the outside seemed in good condition, though underneath the hood it was anything but, as the countless repair bills Pappy juggled would attest. While the three of us waited for the light to change colors, I became transfixed by the jittery figure of a long, thin black woman in a stained T-shirt and sweatpants, a greasy scarf wrapped around her head. She was holding an inconsolable baby in one hand and puffing on a long cigarette with the other, stalking the second-floor balcony of a beat-up old Victorian mansion that had been converted into apartments.

I must have really been staring at her, because all of a sudden I noticed that she wasn't aimlessly pacing back and forth anymore but pointing and yelling specifically at our car. "What the fuck are you staring at?" she howled. "You rich, white motherfuckers in your Murr-say-*deez*, go the fuck home! You think you can just come and watch us like you in a goddamn zoo?"

She was making a scene. Passersby in the street were taking notice and looking at our car, too. That was a time when Benzes were the shit and you had to be careful where you parked because tough guys would pull off the little hood ornament and wear it from a chain around their necks—ready-made jewelry. I was terribly uncomfortable being the center of attention there in that backseat, mentally pleading for the light to turn green. I was also confused as hell. Who were these white people this woman kept referring to? Was she talking about ... *us*—was she talking about *me*? Of course my mother was white, but I didn't understand how she could think *I* was white, too. After all, I was on the way that very moment to have my hair cut at the only barbershop in the area that would cut hair like mine—curly, nappy hair. The kind that "didn't move," the kind of hair that disqualified me from getting cuts at the white barbershop two blocks from my house. But this woman *was* talking to me.

"Just ignore her," my mother said, and finally we drove away. But I couldn't drive that woman's angry face out of my head. She had somehow stripped me of myself, taken something from me. I felt I had to protect myself from ever feeling that kind of loss again.

When I stepped into the barbershop that day and every second Saturday afterward, I was extra careful to pay attention to the other black boys sitting inside, some with their uncles, some with their fathers and brothers, some sitting all alone. These boys became like models to me. I studied their postures and their screwfaces, the unlaced purple and turquoise Filas on their feet, their mannerisms, the way they slapped hands in the street. These boys would never be singled out and dissed the way I had been. I decided I wanted whatever it was that protected them.

Inside Unisex, it smelled deliciously of witch hazel and Barbasol, and there were three long rows of cushioned seats facing five swiveling barber's chairs like bleachers in a gymnasium. There was an old, fake-wood-paneled color television suspended from the ceiling in the far back corner. If a bootlegged movie wasn't playing on the VCR, the TV stayed stuck on one channel in particular the rest of the time, a channel I soon learned was called Black Entertainment Television. At the time in the morning when I usually came into the shop, the program *Rap City* would be showing. These barbershop *Rap City* sessions were not my first exposure to hip-hop music and culture, of course; I had been aware of it vaguely through the tapes my brother brought home and played in his bedroom. I don't believe, though, that I had ever noticed BET before, and in the strange, homogeneously black setting of Unisex Hair Creationz and the city of Plainfield beyond it, the sight of this all-black cable station mesmerized and awed me. Watching BET felt cheap and even a little wrong on an intuitive level—my parents wouldn't admire most of what was shown; Pappy called it minstrelsy—but the men and women in the videos didn't just contend for my attention, they demanded it, and I obliged them. They were all so luridly sexual, so gaudily decked out, so physically confident with an oh-I-wish-a-nigga-would air of defiance, so defensively assertive, I couldn't pry my eyes away.

One morning, Ice-T's "New Jack Hustler" video came on, and though I didn't know the meaning behind the title—or even whether I liked what I was hearing—I knew for sure that the other boys in the shop didn't seem to question any of it, and I sensed that I shouldn't, either. All of them knew the words to the song and some rapped along to it convincingly. I paid attention to the slang they were using and decided I had better learn it myself. Terms like "nigga" and "bitch" were embedded in my thought process, and I was consciously aware for the first time that it wasn't enough just to know the lexicon. There was also a certain way of moving and gesticulating that went with whatever was being said, a silent body language that everybody seemed to speak and understand, whether rapping or chatting, which I would need to get down, too. Over the weeks and months that followed, as I became more and more adept at mimicking and projecting blackness the BET way, and while it was all still fresh to me, what struck me most about this new behavior was how far it veered not just from that of my white classmates and friends at Holy Trinity, but also from that of my father and the two older black barbers in the barbershop—sharp men who looked out of place in Unisex and who held the door and brushed parts on the sides of their heads.

One afternoon I came home from the barbershop sporting an aerodynamic new hair creation of my own. "What on earth did you let them do to you, son?" Pappy said as soon as he saw me. (Our house was not spacious; the front door opened directly into Pappy's study, which he had converted from what ordinarily would have been a living room. To enter the house was literally to step into his scrutinizing gaze.)

"Huh?" I said, touching my hand to my head. The top was so flat and cylindrical it resembled an unused No. 2 pencil eraser; the sides and the back were shaved all the way down, revealing a shaft of high-yellow scalp.

"What, they didn't listen when you told them what you wanted?"

"No, they did," I said. "This is what I wanted."

"You wanted *that*?"

"Well, yeah, it's what everyone is wearing, Babe; it's what's on

BET and in all the magazines." (We call my father Babe when speaking to him casually, kind of a *tu* to the *vous* of Pappy.)

"And you want to look like everyone else, son? Is that what you want?" He was staring at me intently now.

I stood there before him, studying the Air Flights on my feet. I didn't have a response he would find remotely respectable. The thing is that I *did* want to look like everyone else—everyone else in the barbershop and on that TV screen. After all, even in the backseat of a big ol' Murrsaydeez, the woman on the balcony would never mistake a brother with a flattop like *this* for being white.

Annoyed or dismayed by my new coif as he was, though, Pappy allowed Clarence and me a generous amount of latitude when it came to our personal style, as long as we were giving him our best efforts in what he cared about most: the development of our minds. What this meant, giving him our best, was not that we were pressured to place first in our classes or even to get straight A's on our schoolwork, although it would have been welcome if we did. We were expected to maintain decent grades, but it was deeper than that. Pappy, no longer working as a sociologist, now put his PhD and extensive store of personal knowledge and reading to use running a private academic and SAT preparation service from our home. From the second grade on, giving Pappy our best meant we needed to try hard in school, but much more important than that, we needed to study one-on-one with him in the evenings and on the weekends, on long vacations, and all throughout the summer break. If we could not do that, he was able to make our home the most uncomfortable inn to lodge in. When Clarence began blowing off work, he didn't just get grounded, he came home to find his bedroom walls stripped bare, his Michael Jordan and Run-D.M.C.

posters replaced with pastel sheets of algebra equations Pappy had printed out and tacked up.

As for me, the first time Pappy called me into his study to explain my summer schedule, I was seven and my eyes betrayed me, welling with tears against my will. When he looked up from his notes and saw this, he got so offended that he stormed out of the room and I fell into my mother's lap crying. I did not want to do the work he had planned for me. I wanted to play with my friends and have sleepover parties. I wanted to capture fireflies in ventilated Smucker's jars and beat Super Mario Brothers on Clarence's Nintendo. That was the truth. However, more than anything, I wanted not to disappoint my father. With my mother's encouragement and some Kleenex, I followed Pappy into his bedroom and told him that I had just had something in my eye and that, in fact, I had not been crying. I was eager to start studying, I told him. He suspended his disbelief and led me back to his desk, where he proceeded to lay out an intensive program of regimented work in syllogistic and spatial reasoning, vocabulary-building, Miller analogies, arithmetic, and reading comprehension—his signature cocktail.

If Pappy was a tyrant, he was a gentle and conflicted one, who did not relish the role. He yearned for a time when he would cease having to be one at all. What he hoped was that if he could somehow just make reading and studying appealing enough to his boys, eventually we wouldn't need his prodding anymore and we'd simply do it on our own. To that end, he made sure not just to dangle punishment over our heads, Sword of Damocles–style, and leave it at that. He went out of his way to be fair. If we just did what he asked without too much complaint, he would do us some real solids in return, such as paying us generously for our time ("Studying is your job, and an honest day's work deserves an honest day's pay"), intervening on our behalf when our mother doled out chores ("Studying is their *only* job"), and tolerating a slew of hair, clothing, and dating choices that were in flagrant violation of his personal tastes.

Despite these enticements, Clarence would always find it difficult to take to long periods of study, and he went through fits of resistance routinely. Being the younger brother, I had the advantage of learning from his mistakes and avoiding most of his battles. I was what Pappy called a "dutiful son." Most of the time this dutifulness of mine sufficed. We were rarely in open conflict with each other, and he was almost always patient and playfully encouraging with me.

"Thomas Chatterton," he'd say, addressing me by my middle name as I sped through his study on my way to the kitchen, oblivious to my surroundings. "Do you know you wear the name of a brilliant poet, son?" he'd call from the other room.

"Yeah, of course, Babe," I'd say, poking my head into the refrigerator, looking for something sweet.

"And do you know they call him the Marvelous Boy, his poetry was so fine?" he'd say, still talking to me from the other room.

"Uh-uh," I'd say with my mouth full.

"Well, they do. His poetry was so fine, in fact, and he was so young when he wrote it, that the adults couldn't even believe the work was his own. They all accused him of copying someone else, someone much older."

"They did?"

"They sure did. And do you know that he became so distraught by this, he became so discouraged, that he killed himself when he was only seventeen years old? He decided he couldn't live with the dishonor."

"That's horrible."

"Yes it is, son. Life is not fair. But now you're going to bring *honor* to his name, aren't you? It's very important that you do that, son."

"But I don't know how to, Babe," I'd say, returning to the study with a bowl of ice cream or a glass of soda in my hand.

"Well, you don't have to be a poet, son. You can be a great philosopher, for example—pull up a seat."

"A philosopher?" I'd say, and sit down.

"Yes, in fact, you're a philosopher already, aren't you?"

"I don't think so," I'd say, my cheeks flushing.

"Well, yes you are, son. Think about it: Do you question the things around you? Do you reflect on their meaning? Are you interested in the truth?"

"Yeah."

"Then you're a philosopher, son," he would tell me, and I would laugh, embarrassed because I didn't feel at all like a philosopher, whatever that was I could only imagine. I felt ignorant, which is what I confessed to him. And he would tell me that ignorance is the beginning of knowledge and talk of men named Socrates and Confucius. He revered these two men perhaps above all other men, Socrates for his edict to know thyself and Confucius for his devotion to learning and personal excellence, he said. I would sit there at Pappy's desk, exhausting whatever sugary collation I had brought with me from the kitchen, and listen to him talk. "Well, I've told you enough," he'd eventually say. "Now, you tell me—how am

I going to grow up and be smart like you?" We'd laugh and I'd try to come up with some reply. These questioning talks I had with Pappy were so frequent in my childhood that to this day the name Socrates remains mingled in my mind with the image of my balding and bearded father seated in his study. I cannot think of one without inadvertently conjuring the other.

Sometimes, though, Pappy grew impatient waiting for the love of learning to take root in me. "I don't understand," he'd say in moments of frustration, "how you can keep walking past all these books and never stop to pick up a single one of them. My people told me *not* to read—don't you know what I would have done to have all this? Don't you ever get curious, son?" These were simple, honest questions that sometimes he put to me with a shake of the head and wry smile. Sometimes, though, he didn't smile at all. In these latter moments, the look on his face was nothing like anger and something like pain—a sort of deep, serious pain I have only seen replicated in pictures of black faces of a certain age and demographic. It was a pain that I knew I couldn't have caused but somehow must have mistakenly activated. I would stand there looking at him, frozen, like a deer suspended in halogen beams, and stammer some weak response.

That particular afternoon after my visit to the barbershop, Pappy let drop the subject of my rectangular head of hair and handed me my work for the day. There was no long talk and no sadness in his face that afternoon. "Memory exercises and then vocabulary, both synonyms and antonyms," he said. "Write them all out on flashcards and then come see me."

"OK, Babe," I said, and went to my room carrying a pale green tachistoscope, a stack of SAT and GRE word lists, and a thick

Merriam-Webster's Collegiate Dictionary, glad to have dodged a confrontation. After a morning spent at the barbershop, submerged in Black Entertainment Television, speaking and thinking in my florid second tongue—Ebonics—it was time now to return to the staid and familiar language of my father.

CHAPTER TWO

A Wicked Genie

The ball arced high off the rim, up above the top of the back-board, and over in the direction of the stage, where, on special occasions, we put on concerts for our families. Today was no special occasion, just the end of another Thursday afternoon gym class, a chance to get in a quick game of three-on-three before the final bell rang and my friends and I went home to cartoons and after-school snacks. Mr. Moustafa, the strict Egyptian phys ed instructor, stood on the far side of the auditorium, a white shirt tucked into loose black sweatpants, his back to the half of the court we occupied, guiding a group of uncoordinated girls through the motions of double Dutch. Craig and I sprinted together toward the long rebound, both putting hands on the ball at the very same time. Naturally more inclined to acts of aggression than me, at once Craig tugged hard at the ball. I bent my knees and held on firm, lurching forward and then drawing him back toward me, the ball tight between our chests. Our eyes met as we both registered that he had just failed in his attempt to wrench it loose from me. *You're a nigger, too, Thomas, aren't you?* I could hear him say as I took in his dark blue eyes and that stupid blond sugar bowl rimming his face. I stepped forward into Craig and the ball as hard as I could and let go of both of them. He stumbled backward and the edge of the stage jammed into the rear of his rib cage. He collapsed, coughing for breath. A freckled boy named Sean, the spitting image of the *MAD* magazine mascot, ran over to Craig while the other boys stood off to the side. "You OK, Craig?" Craig was red in the face, wheezing, but nodded in the affirmative. "Jesus, what'd you do that for, Thomas?" Sean said, looking up at me.

"'Cause I felt like it, bitch—what the fuck *you* gonna do about it?" I said, molding my face into my best rendition of the kind of mean mug I had been seeing a lot of on Saturdays in Plainfield. I had never said anything like that before to anyone, and I felt strange doing it. If either Craig or Sean would have just gone across the gym to Mr. Moustafa and told on me, I would have repented right then and there. As it turned out, though, and to my surprise, neither of them did any such thing. We were all about ten years old and roughly the same strength and size. But they just shrank and walked away from me, as though I were somehow much bigger than that. That was so damn *easy*, I thought to myself. When the bell rang, I gathered my things and walked off, too.

Those days, as I was learning to project a certain kind of blackness, I was also coming to understand that it is not simply a means of protection—it can be a real weapon, too. There is an undeniably seductive power that black boys who grow up around white boys and pay attention can exploit in the state of nature that is grade school and the playground. Of course, this kind of power is the power of Caliban, but as a child, I didn't know that sort of thing. All I knew was this: If they, the white boys, found me, the black boy, credibly black enough, everything was gravy.

Where I lived there was really nothing blacker you could do than shoot hoops. Luckily for me I was pretty good at it, and whenever I was free from schoolwork or studying I would play. I began taking the Wilson ball that Pappy had given me and going by myself over to the courts at Forest Road Park, down the street from our house. We had a basket set up in the driveway that Pappy had bought for us the moment Clarence and I first expressed interest in the game, but most of the time I preferred to use the park rims instead. In the driveway there was just basketball, and that was all; at the park there was basketball plus everything else that went along with it. The culture and the politics, you could say, were in the park.

One day I was there shooting one thousand short-range jump shots: five hundred from the left elbow, five hundred from the right. It was a routine I had picked up at one of the basketball camps Pappy sent Clarence and me to each summer. I was up on the elevated secondary courts shooting and keeping an eye on the main court below, where a big-time five-on-five was under way. RaShawn was playing down there, and he was like a star to me. He was neither tall nor short, but I thought he was good-looking—the way I wanted to look at his age. He had his shirt off and was wearing loose jeans and black-and-blue Air Maxes (the ones that I wanted).

He was muscular and fit and had been sipping from a large bottle of Olde English 800 before the game began. Everyone knew RaShawn. He was a year or two ahead of Clarence in school, but he seemed much older than that to me. The last time I saw him, he had bought my friends and me Italian ices from the green-and-white Penguin truck. He didn't go up to the truck and buy them for us or anything like that; he peeled off bills from a knot in his pocket, as thick and layered as a Spanish onion, and said, "Go get an icey if you want one." I thought so much of him after that, when I got home I told my mother I was going to give my children *real* black names like RaShawn or Ramiq or Jamal, not white ones like Thomas.

On this particular day he didn't seem to recognize me when I called out to him, "Yo, RaShawn!" The game was intense, though, and I thought that maybe I'd be able to catch his eye when it was over, once everyone took a break to walk to the water fountain by the tennis courts and he retreated to his malt liquor over on the bench. Some of the players in the game I recognized as members of the local high school varsity team. RaShawn was not on any team, I knew, but nevertheless it was clear that he was the best player on the blacktop. He could jump so high. He'd already caught one breakaway dunk (a slick reverse). I took another shot. When I looked back up, there was a pause in the action down below and the ball was bouncing uphill toward where I stood.

"I said get the ball, ma'fucker!" RaShawn said to a tall and well-built white boy in a blue-and-white Scotch Plains Raiders tank top who was slowly backpedaling away from him. The white boy had just about a head on RaShawn and probably thirty pounds, too. RaShawn was closing the gap between the two of them almost imperceptibly.

"It was off you. I ain't gettin' the ball," the white boy said to RaShawn, or he said something that amounted to the same thing.

RaShawn didn't say anything, kept walking; the other boy kept backpedaling; all three courts were watching. Someone else said, "Yo, it's no big deal, I'll go get the ball." All of a sudden there was no more space separating the two players and RaShawn was beating on the white boy savagely. I had never seen someone be hit like that in real life, and it was the sound that surprised me most—much louder than I would have expected.

The first blow came so quickly, the white boy didn't have time to get a hand up and it landed squarely on his jaw. His knees buckled and he started to sway, but RaShawn tagged him three or four more times in the face, chest, and gut before letting him fall. He hit the ground, by all signs unconscious. As he lay there, motionless, RaShawn stomped, kicked, and field-goaled him in the face, ribs, and back. The kick to the back sounded like the beat of a war drum. No one in the park muttered a word of protest or attempted to come to the boy's defense. Then the weirdest thing happened: RaShawn curtailed the ass-whipping of his own volition, went and got the ball himself, and said, "Six-five, y'all ball." A guy on the sideline stepped in to replace the fallen white boy, and the game resumed as if it had never stopped.

I don't know what happened next or how the white boy recovered and got himself out of the park, because I didn't stick around long enough to find out. I gathered my things and left the courts as quickly and surreptitiously as I could, without waiting to speak to RaShawn and without drawing attention to myself and looking like a bitch in front of the older black boys. I was so preoccupied with the latter concern, in fact, that I forgot my new Nike Windbreaker on the grass. By the time I went back to search for it that evening, it had been stolen and there was no one left on the court to question either about the jacket's whereabouts or the fight that had taken place earlier. Back at home, however, my thoughts weren't dominated by what I had lost but by what I had seen. I was as in awe of RaShawn as I was terrified of him. In a certain way, I think that I was proud of him. He was as hard as Ice-T or NWA or Kool G Rap or any of those brothers I had seen on BET, and I was sure that no white kid would ever dream of calling *him* a monkey to his face or asking why his hair didn't move.

The more I reflected on RaShawn, the more I pulled apart the imagery of that day's events and melded it with memories of my own confrontation with Craig, the more I began to realize something: The loose jeans falling from our hips, the unlaced kicks adorning our feet, the slang encrypting our speech, the slow roll choreographing our strides, the funky-ass hairstyles embellishing our domes, the hip-hop soundtracking our days, the pigment darkening our skin (whether octoroon or fully black)—all these disparate elements congealed into a kind of glue that invisibly but definitively united people like RaShawn and me. As different as the two of us were, it was undeniable that we shared something with each other that neither of us had in common with either Craig or that white boy stretched out on the asphalt. What that meant, I suspected, was that I, too, could participate in some of the immense power that brothers like RaShawn wielded and exercised all over the place. It was a wicked genie that I, too, could summon if I chose, if I was just willing to play down the things I saw in my father's study—things that only put distance between RaShawn and me—and to play up the things I saw on BET, on the street, and on ESPN. It was easy enough to do that.

There were very few other black children at Holy Trinity with me, which meant that there existed scarcely any authority or context against which my evolving self could be measured or fact-checked. The more I channeled my inner RaShawn and aped whatever I saw on Rap City and SportsCenter, the more I noticed that the white kids I went to school with were willing to buy into the 'hood persona I was busy developing. They entered into our little social contract ready to enable my street fantasies and to cede me the physical sphere entirely. My classmates took for granted that I would beat them in the hundred-yard dash, hit them with killer crossovers, and pluck rebounds from up above their heads. The idea that I couldn't dance was met with incredulity, and in the locker room everybody operated on the assumption that black dicks were the biggest. The truth is that a brother can get used to such flattery, and quickly. The result was that I got a big head and allowed myself to sign this tacit agreement with all but my closest white friends. At first, it put some pep in my step. Before long, though, I couldn't help but realize that I was these white boys' superior—yes, perhaps, possibly—but I was not their equal. In the classroom and in terms of material well-being for example, their expectations of me tended to be much lower than of themselves and each other. The same Tina who had puzzled over the rigidity of my hair revealed herself to be equally perplexed when I caught a higher grade than she did on a history exam. My friend Mark, apropos of nothing, asked me one day whether I had ever seen a house as spacious as his before. When we went upstairs to dinner, a nice roast served with steamed vegetables, he wanted to know if I got to eat that way at home.

At first, these aspects of the deal were insulting to me—my natural proclivity was to take offense here: Why couldn't I be smart and middle-class, too, I thought (albeit with a wicked left hook and an enviably sized penis, of course)? But gradually, gradually, like a desert of sand sifting through a monstrous hourglass, after days and weeks and months and years of these constant asymmetric relations, fronting like I came from the ghetto when I was around kids like Mark and Tina seemed a small and even reasonable price to pay for the obeisance I could be granted in return. Anyway, none of the black kids I met in the barbershop and on the basketball courts had ever shown signs of giving a damn about being book smart or leading unadventurous middle-class lives. "I'ma be a nigga for life," my ten-year-old friend Justin told me proudly. "All that other shit is for the crackers." Like Justin, the rest of the black kids I knew just acted like ghetto fabulous street superstars, hurling themselves like Kamikazes into the world of hip-hop, sports, and gangster fantasy that we saw reflected around the 'hood and on TV, and that we heard on the radio. They had been defining themselves all along through their bodies and not their minds, which is something I had begun to do as well when I was out of my father's reach. It was a simple carrot-and-stick situation between the two groups—the whites had plenty of carrots to give an athletic wannabe thug, and I could still feel the lash of that thin black woman's stick. I was motivated, and from both sides, to keep shit as real as I possibly could. For very different reasons that in the end amounted to the same reason, it was hard to know for which side failure to do so would be worse.

My brother's problem with the white boys back in second grade, and probably the reason the other black boys didn't defend him, it struck me, was that he hadn't come across as *credibly black enough* when he was tested. I resolved to avoid that mistake. This meant that there were times when I would have to perform.

Late in the seventh grade, I remember walking out of Holy Trinity with Maria, an olive-complexioned girl who was blessed with a head of thick black tresses and a precocious junior high bosom. The two of us, flirting and laughing, came down the front walk to the main street and passed by a group of high school kids loitering on the corner, drinking ectoplasm-green Mountain Dews and smoking cigarettes. One of them, a handsome guy who looked like the singer Jon B. and who was dressed in an oversized Tommy Hilfiger rugby like a typical Jersey wigger, called out something to me. It was probably something designed to impress Maria at my expense (she looked that mature). It was a mild taunt I can't remember now, and one I could have easily brushed aside. But some of my classmates were standing there and heard it, and Maria heard it, and I had so much invested in my own black image at this point that to not respond in a tough manner would have cost me face in a way it would not have cost my white friends. "Why don't you go fuck yourself?" I said to the boy, and kept walking.

Maria giggled, impressed with my bravado. It had been a couple of years since a white boy had asserted himself to me, and I had bought into the myth of my own invincibility around them so thoroughly, so completely, that frankly I didn't expect him to do or say anything further. Of course, he was three or four years older than me, and much stronger, and had ideas of his own. He flipped out and jumped at me.

"Bitch, I'll fuck you up right now!" he screamed, and I knew that if we fought, he would win decisively. His friends stepped between us and explained to him that I was just a kid and to leave it alone, but he was incensed.

"I'ma be here every day waiting for you," he threatened as I moved on and his friends held him back.

The next day after school, to my shock, he really was standing there waiting for me, and when I saw this I went back inside the building and slipped out through the back exit. When I got home, I told Clarence what had happened. He said not to worry about it and that he and Michael, his best friend whom we called our cousin, would pick me up from school the next day.

With my heart in my throat, I watched the street go by from the window of my last-period music class. When the bell was about to ring, Clarence and Michael pulled up in Michael's old navy blue Buick and got out and sat on the hood and lit Black & Milds, from which they took long drags like philosophers and blew dark clouds. One of my classmates turned to me and said, *"Daaaamn."* They were about seventeen years old, Clarence and Michael. Clarence, dressed in a Nike Air T-shirt, a pair of Air Flights with the plastic swoosh tag still attached, and loose baby blue jeans, looked like a bigger, better-built version of me. Michael, at six-foot-five and in full-on army fatigues, Timberland boots, and a forest green skully pulled down low over his eyes, looked like a punk white boy's worst nightmare.

I rushed out of the building with my head up high, searching the street for Jon B. and running up to my brother and my cousin, each of whom dapped me demonstratively as my white classmates gawked from a distance. The three of us waited there for at least a quarter hour as my classmates trickled off one by one. The boy didn't show. "Get in the car; we gonna find that ma'fucker," Michael said. We drove first past the high school then all around downtown Westfield, windows down, knocking Smif-N-Wessun and the Originoo Gunn Clappaz, not talking. Just as I was losing hope that we would ever settle this score, I saw money emerge with a group of friends from a pizzeria across the street from the train station. Michael swerved to a stop.

"You go up to him, Thomas, and tell him you want to speak with him," he said. "We'll be right behind you."

I got out of the car and approached the boy from behind with a mouth so dry it was like I had sucked on a fistful of cotton balls. "Yo, let me talk to you," I called to him in an unsteady, wildly pubescent voice. He turned around, and when he saw it was me, his face gave way to a theater of emotions—first surprise and then anger and then fear. Fear, ultimately, because he saw Michael and Clarence looming behind me. Before I could say anything further, Michael said, "Yo, are you the bitch that's been coming around fucking with my little man?"

The boy swallowed hard.

"I didn't do shit, he started popping off with me," he said, trying to cop a plea as his friends came over to ask what was going on.

"Y'all might as well keep on walking home," Michael said to

them, "'cause y'all ain't about to do shit right here." To my amazement and probably to the boy's, too, his friends turned around and left.

"What's your name?" Michael said to the boy.

"Bobby."

"Bobby?"

"Uh-huh."

"Walk over to my car, Bobby," Michael said, and Bobby obeyed. Then Michael stepped around to the trunk and opened it, and inside there was a wooden Louisville Slugger and a big white tube sock. "Look into the trunk, bitch," Michael said, and he picked up the sock by the open end and let it dangle from his hand. It had a large bulge weighting down the bottom, which Michael explained to Bobby was a padlock. "Which would you prefer," Michael asked, "that I beat your faggot ass black-and-blue with this padlock or with that Louisville Slugger?" Bobby, alone on the corner with the three of us and deserted by his friends, didn't say anything, just started to cry—to sob, really, in big heaving breaths like he was hyperventilating or suffering from the severest case of hiccups. He looked as if his bowels might move.

"Oh, that's how it is, son? You want to cry now? You want to cry like a little pussy now, Bobby? I thought you was bad, I thought you was tough, I thought you was a gangsta, Bobby?" Michael said, cocking his head to the side, dwarfing Bobby and grilling him in the eyes.

Bobby was sniffling uncontrollably, his face bathed in tears.

"I tell you what, faggot," Michael said, "you apologize to my nigga right now, you say you're sorry and that you fucked up, and I might not take your teeth home with me today."

"I'm sorry, yo . . . , I'm sorry, I'm sorry," Bobby said in between sniffles and wiping his face with the sleeve of his Nautica shirt.

"Tell him whether you accept his faggot-ass apology or not, Thomas," Michael said, turning to me, then turning to Bobby: "Because if he don't accept it, Bobby, you just gonna have to try harder, bitch."

"It's cool," I said, almost feeling bad for the kid. Then Michael ordered Bobby to bounce, but not before warning him that if this conversation were to take place a second time, it wouldn't be verbal. As Bobby thanked Michael and turned to walk away, Clarence flicked the butt of his Black & Mild off the side of Bobby's head and an explosion of orange and gray ash burst from Bobby's hair like a tiny volcano.

The thing is, around other black kids, Clarence and Michael were not particularly tough. In fact, around other black kids like RaShawn, they weren't tough at all. They liked to play video games, play racing games, build radio-controlled cars, watch comedies, and daydream about opening their own nightclub where they would play freestyle and house music and where Clarence would handle all the numbers and Michael would be the life of the party. They were typical suburban teenagers who ate at T.G.I. Friday's on Fridays and haunted the Woodbridge or Menlo Park malls on Saturdays, looking for fast food and fast girls to whom they might dole out their beeper numbers. They bagged groceries at ShopRite and Foodtown after school to put gas in their tanks. Neither of them had ever put a Louisville Slugger or anything approaching one upside another human body. In other words, they were not street kids in even the most liberal sense, but they were conversant (Michael more than Clarence) in their culture.

The way the Puerto Rican kids I knew growing up learned to sway their hips back and forth, the way the Jewish kids learned to recite the Torah, the way the Irish and Italian kids learned to talk like casual bigots, the way the Chinese kids learned to obliterate their schoolwork, that was the way we black kids learned to imitate thugs and gangsters. Around non-blacks, this made us seem hard. Around other blacks, it just made us seem normal.

About a year after my encounter with Bobby, during the summer before I went to high school, Pappy—by this time an older man with bad knees, a thick salt-and-pepper beard, and a powerful-looking bald head—took off from work, packed up our sedan, and drove me down Interstate 95 to Emmitsburg, Maryland, same as he did every year. There he dropped me off at Morgan Wootten's sleep-away basketball camp. Two weeks later, he was back early in the morning to catch the last day of league games and the awards ceremony that followed. My team had advanced to the championship game and, as the starting point guard, I was up for the Most Outstanding Player trophy in my age group.

As we formed layup lines and began to warm up for the game, Pappy made his way across the gym, limping slightly, a book tucked under his arm. He quietly took a seat in the bleachers close by and began to read, underlining as he went along, looking up over his bifocals at the court every now and again. Unlike some of the other dads at these games, Pappy was no yeller; he didn't cheer or even applaud. He also wasn't distracted, constantly checking a pager or stepping out of the gym to make phone calls. His focus was his son, and his thoughtful, stoic presence had the dual-edged effect of motivating and terrifying me. I had grown up understanding that my father—who hadn't known his own father and was the only son of an unwed and uneducated teenage mother who never really recovered from her fall from grace—had triumphed against daunting odds. At his "colored" high school in Galveston he had boxed, debated, played pitcher on the baseball team, played point guard on the basketball team, and played quarterback on the football team. He was his class's homecoming king *and* valedictorian. To him, life itself was competitive, and there was no consolation in placing second. Life was also incredibly fragile, and it only took one misstep to lose it all—that is what his mother's example had taught him—so from childhood on he took everything seriously and made it his mission to always be on point.

My parents told me a story that encapsulates Pappy's paternal psychology completely. As a baby, I was with my mother in our old home in Newark, crawling freely while she was trying to clean and watch after my very active five-year-old brother. We were upstairs, on the second floor of the house. At one end of the room, there was a door that led out into the hallway and down a long flight of carpeted stairs onto the parlor level, where my father had his study and received visitors. I was a quiet baby, and it wouldn't have been odd for me to not be making much noise as I crawled. Somehow, my mother had gotten distracted with my brother, and I made my way over to the door, which wasn't properly closed. I got out into the hallway and soon began tumbling down the staircase in a bright blue bundle of diapers and pajamas, rushing toward the hardwood floor below. As my mother gaped from the landing above, the door to my father's study flew open and out dove Pappy to catch me like a fly ball before I reached the ground. He had been in the middle of a meeting when suddenly he hopped up, told his guests to wait, and bolted to the door. He almost certainly saved my life that morning.

"How in the world did you even hear that?" one of the stunned guests asked him afterward.

"I've been listening for that sound from the moment we brought the baby home from the hospital," Pappy said.

I grew up knowing that no matter where I was or what I was doing, Pappy never stopped listening for the sound of me falling.

As I glanced over at him from the court, I shifted back and forth in my box-fresh Air Jordans, adjusting my sagged-just-so mesh shorts for the twentieth time. I alternated between fussing with my headband and feigning an insouciant pose. When my turn came and I caught the ball on the right side of the key, I took two hard, deliberate dribbles and slashed to the basket, finger rolling the ball and slapping the glass with the same hand for effect. The ball hung on the rim and spun out. Pappy, looking over his book, shook his head and beckoned me over to the sideline.

"Son, just play your game," he said, putting his hand on my shoulder. "Leave all that foolishness and showmanship behind, and don't let me or anyone else get you nervous. Stay cool, and listen to the sound of your own drummer. Tick, tick, tick, tick, count it out in your head; make your own rhythm." He gave me nuggets of counsel like this whenever I had to compete, whether I was running track, playing basketball, or taking a test. This time, though, he added something else, something I did not understand: "If you're going to compete," he said, locking onto my eyes for emphasis, "then do your best, son, always do your best, but remember that I really don't care if we *ever* have another black athlete or entertainer."

I won that Most Outstanding Player trophy that year, and Pappy was pleased despite what he had said to me on the bleachers. On the ride home, he gave me a choice: I could either go to Delbarton, a lily-white and regionally prestigious boys' school far from our house and even farther from our price range, where he believed he could secure me a scholarship, or I could go down the street to Union Catholic, a not-prestigious-at-all parochial school, but one with a voluptuous brown student body. The decision was mine, Pappy said, because truth be told, he couldn't bring himself to force a boy to go to school without girls, simple as that.

Besides, it wasn't as if he trusted either institution to educate me as he saw fit. Wherever I went, in the evenings after school, on weekends, and in the summers I would still have to study one-on-one with him—same as I always had. I knew that I could make the team at either school, so I leaped at the opportunity, finally, to surround myself with other black kids—specifically black girls—and chose to go to Union Catholic.

CHAPTER THREE

What About Your Friends?

I was standing at my locker one morning when a tall, thickset girl named Takira came flying down the hallway like a whirling dervish. "Y'all, you know what day it is today, right?" she said, panting.

"No, what?" someone asked.

"It's the anniversary of Biggie's death, y'all," she said.

"Oh, true," someone else said.

"Word, throw down some ice for the nicest MC, yo," said another with an air of solemnity.

"Make sure you remember to keep him in your prayers, everybody, for real," Takira said as the bell rang for first period and we each went our separate ways. I think I heard someone say that they missed him.

Even as a teenager immersed in *Yo! MTV Raps,* the absurdity of this exchange nagged at me. Here we were, a bunch of young black private-school kids, not wealthy but also not poor, who were unable to identify the year (the decade?) that W.E.B. Du Bois or Thurgood Marshall died, and who could not say for certain the date of Martin Luther King's birth without the aid of a calendar—and this only because it was also a day off from school—yet here we were, serious as cancer when it came to things like sanctifying the anniversary of "the assassination of Biggie Smalls." And like our parents' generation with Dr. King, we knew exactly where we were the moment we learned the rapper had died. (I was on the couch in my bedroom, talking on the phone.) Everybody assembled at this impromptu B.I.G. vigil could recite at will whole songs and interludes from *Ready to Die* and *Life After Death,* and I was no exception. I was just as besotted with Biggie as my classmates were. Yet I was also torn between allegiance to the fallen drug dealer and something else—something coming from deep in the back of my head or in my conscience. I knew for an irrefutable fact that none of the other kids I was looking at had ever managed to crease the spine of *The Autobiography of Malcolm X* or *The Souls of Black Folk*. I'd only creased them myself because Pappy made me. Toni Morrison, if anything, triggered some blurry image of Oprah Winfrey in our minds. No one, including me, could put a finger on the difference between a Miles Davis number and one by John Coltrane or Thelonious Monk. We were as ignorant of jazz as we were of the blues or black literature. Most of us could not say who the key figures of the Harlem Renaissance were. Thoughts like these flickered in my mind as I listened to Takira, and for a second—for the flash of a second, as I studied the gravity of expression playing across my classmates' faces—I felt a pang of shame as I heard Pappy's voice say, *Son, I don't care if we ever have another black entertainer.* In that moment I knew that he was right.

Most of the time, however, I did not question what I saw or heard. Hip-hop style and culture governed everything at Union Catholic, same as it did on the playground and in the barbershop, and by this point I didn't just do as the locals did—I was a proper Roman when in Rome. I ceased entirely to hang out with the white kids I knew from Holy Trinity and plunged myself like a diver into an all-black-and-Latino social circle. Some of my new friends were middle-class like me and some had parents and grandparents and aunts and uncles who busted their asses to get their children's asses bused out of the working-class and inner-city communities in which they lived. Most of these latter students came from places that were tougher than burlap, places that made the local news, such as Plainfield, Irvington, and Newark—small cities where the public school systems were failing and students entered their school buildings through metal detectors.

When the kids commuting from these areas arrived each morning in sleepy Scotch Plains, they assumed a prestigious role in my eyes: They were messengers of authenticity, ambassadors of blackness. One of the most popular, Jerome, was a short, well-barbered, and raspy-voiced boy with a strut, whose fourteen-year-old face wore a considerably older expression. His big brother belonged to a rap group that was down with the Fugees. Jerome was more of a lunch-table rapper, but he knew his role and played it well and got tons of props for the effort. He may have had to be shuttled away from the indignities of hard living back in Newark, but here he was aristocracy. He could punctuate a double-clutch handshake with a finger snap or greet you with a head nod followed by a nonchalant "Whatup, my nigga?" He smoked blunts and drank 40s in the ninth grade. His "chinky" eyes stayed bloodshot.

On the surface, it would seem that he and I had nothing in common: I had a stable, two-parent household where my biggest concern was not to let my father down; he could stay up until three or four in the morning on a weeknight and come and go from school sky-high, smelling like Indonesia, without a book bag on his shoulders. We had been raised differently, but what united us and the rest of our peers wasn't our home environments or even simply the color of our skin: It was our deep identification with the culture of hip-hop—it was that invisible glue.

At the end of school each day, I'd wish that I were on one of the all-black Newark-bound buses instead of being banished to the local bus or the passenger seat of my mother's car. When class let out, as the different buses idled in the parking lot—some destined for Piscataway and some for Rahway, Elizabeth, or East Orange, all filling with rowdy cargo—the boisterous sounds of Hot 97 FM leaked out of the half-ajar windows on the Newark-bound side. A perpetual party was happening over there; kids were dancing on their seats. It was a dance that I was unable to attend.

I doubt the students on those buses felt they were missing out on anything over on my end. I don't think Jerome, the self-styled "Brick City Representer," or many of the others would have cared to switch places with me on the local bus. After all, there was nothing "real" about the way I kept my afternoons. I would be buried in a Barron's Test Prep book before Jerome's key would touch the latch. This was incompatible with the spirit of the environment we inhabited, where being black meant having lots of rhythm and chat, but nothing more than a passing interest in getting good marks.

There was, however, one boy who, to my surprise, did want to join me on that local bus. I had become best friends at UC with a boy named Charles. Charles was the most popular student in my class, a short kid, but tough. He had brown, laughing eyes and a head he kept bald as a baby's. In his clear, caramel skin there fraternized the Indian, the conquistador, and the slave. He was "cock-diesel," my brother said, meaning he was strong as hell. I had never met a prouder or more magnetic person in my life. Charles began coming over to my house every day after school, and Pappy would treat him like another son. The two of us, Charles and I, came to depend on each other in a mutually beneficial way, though at the time I never would have put it in such terms. With me, and by that I mean with Pappy, Charles gained entrée into the SAT/college prep boot camp ("training" he called it) that was my homelife since the second grade; with Charles, I got an implicit endorsement from the coolest kid in school, a permanent seat at the Plainfield-, Irvington-, and Newark-occupied tables in the lunchroom as well as a vouchsafe against my sometimes too-proper diction and manners. Plus, having Charles around the house just made the work I already had to do less grueling, less of a chore.

There was nothing strange about Pappy taking in one of my friends this way. When he was young, Pappy had dreamed of becoming a physician. "I guess you could say I've always wanted to be a healer," he would tell us. Over the years, he has reached out to almost all of Clarence's and my friends and tried to heal them in one way or another. That was how he was, willing to help and to teach, to heal and encourage anyone. One of my brother's foul Italian friends, Frankie, had come to the house once and Pappy asked him how he was doing in school. He told Pappy that he'd gotten an A on a test. I doubted that story, but Pappy reached into his pocket and took out what loose cash he had—a ten, a five, a couple of ones—and handed it over to Frankie, telling him that he was proud of his work and to keep it up.

We were never poor, but at the time, with both Clarence and me in private school and no health care (whenever one of us got sick, Pappy paid the doctor in cash), money could be so tight that ice cream was a luxury. "Why," I said to Pappy after Frankie had left, "would you give that piece of trash a dime?" Pappy just removed his glasses, rubbing the area around his temples where the too-tight stems burrowed into his flesh, and looked at me with weary eyes, as if I'd asked him the simplest and most obvious question he'd heard in his life.

"Because, son, maybe no one else ever has," he said. Then he looked into the kitchen: "Kathy, what do we have to eat for dinner?"

Pappy was nobody's fool; there's not a Panglossian bone in his body. He knew exactly what kind of kid Frankie was. It's just that he believed above all in the power of the will—that it is never too late to make a change if the will is in it. And who could know what encouragement might stick with whom and when? Certainly not him, he thought, and so he refused to discriminate. He tried to heal everyone the same. Charles was the only one of our friends who had ever been willing or up for it. The rest, including Frankie, just thought Pappy was a crazy old man or they acted like he was the dentist and kept their distance.

Anyway, Charles would come over to my house after school and the three of us would pull up chairs at Pappy's book-piled desk and gobble down foot-long submarine sandwiches, potato chips, and cans of Dr. Brown's black cherry soda before my mother came home from work and made dinner. We would laugh and shoot the shit about anything—women, basketball, God (Pappy had walked out of church when he was nine years old, and no amount of beatings from his aunt's belt could induce him back inside), truth, racism, the fries at McDonald's and Wendy's (whose were more flavorful?). When we had exhausted the topic at hand, whatever it was, Charles and I would clear away the remnants of the meal and study math, or analogical reasoning, or chess openings and defenses. Pappy saw life as one really long chess match, a series of veiled gambits; you needed a strategy, a plan. One wrong move meant *checkmate*—especially if your pieces happened to be black. Pappy still studied, too. While we did our assignments, he would read whatever book it was he was working on that day, which back then could have been anything from Foucault's discourses on power to the complete annotated history of the Byzantine Empire. Some days—these were my favorites—we just spent hours memorizing lists of vocabulary words like "eschatological" and "sesquipedalian," quizzing each other at the kitchen table before Pappy drilled us on their antonymic meanings. The goal for me then—just as it had been when I was a teary-eyed seven-year-old—was not so much to learn as to impress and please Pappy. That was what mattered most. Charles adored Pappy, too, although like me he never dreamed of telling anybody back at school what it was we were up to in those afternoons and evenings in Fanwood. The other kids all assumed that we were playing video games or working out or doing jack shit. It was easier for us to let them think that.

One afternoon it happened to be a collection of Shirley Jackson's short stories that Pappy was thumbing through. As Charles and I began to study, Pappy walked over to the Xerox machine in front of the wall that divided the study from the kitchen and started making copies. We always had an industrial-strength Xerox machine in the house. Pappy photocopied everything, from receipts to vocabulary lessons to important newspaper articles and poems; he photocopied copies of photocopies, which over the years began to accumulate in every room, like sawdust in a sawmill.

"Before you boys get into your work today," he said, "I want you to read something for me and to think about it." With that, he plopped down in front of us a handful of sharpened pencils (you can't read without underlining) and two stapled copies of Jackson's "The Lottery," reproduced on a pastel pink paper that had blurred toner marks along the edges.

This was not the first time I had seen the story. Along with Richard Connell's "The Most Dangerous Game," O. Henry's "The Gift of the Magi," and the poem "Invictus" by William Ernest Henley, it belonged to a small idiosyncratic canon of works that Pappy adored and which, as a young boy, I treated with a dutiful if unthinking reverence. An extremely concise tale, "The Lottery" is straightforward enough for a small child to comprehend. The setting is the following: Each year in a mid-twentieth-century rural American village, residents of various adjoining towns conduct compulsory town-wide lotteries. This tradition stretches back as far as the history of the settlements themselves, and the residents have no memories of a time before lotteries. In fact, the ritual is such a natural part of life that they don't give it much thought outside of the two hours annually they devote to the practice. Participating in the lottery, like watching high school football or eating spicy food, is simply something that is done where these people are from.

On the morning of the drawing, a warm June day, the town children run around playing, gathering rocks into piles and stuffing their pockets with pebbles and stones, as their parents and grandparents congregate in the main square. The adults chat and gossip and rumors circulate that one or two neighboring towns have begun to float the idea of doing away with the lottery altogether. In fact, a woman says, some places have already gotten rid of the practice. This is craziness, everyone agrees—a betrayal; the lottery has been going on for as long as anyone can remember—to break with it would be to break with a part of themselves.

When the drawing begins, husbands from each family step forward and pull a folded slip of paper from a battered black box that is older than the oldest living resident. One of the husbands, a man named Bill Hutchinson, draws the winning ticket marked with a black circle, and his family now must participate in a second drawing to determine who of the five of them will be the ultimate winner. It is Bill's wife, Tessie, who pulls the marked slip this time. She becomes frantic and shouts and pleads for a redo—it isn't fair, she cries in vain. The townspeople, including her husband and children, form a circle around her and the first stone strikes her in the head.

"Oh, hell no!" Charles shouted. "I would *never* go for that—I'd go down swinging, or better yet, I'd have left that place ahead of time, moved to one of those other towns where they don't pull that stuff anymore."

"You think so?" Pappy said from his desk. "Well, that can be hard to do when the time comes."

If I wasn't in school or studying with Charles and Pappy, I often hung out and listened to rap music at my friend Sam's house. He was a year younger than me and from one of the two other black families on the white side of town. Naturally, we had been friends for years. Sam's mother was a worldly woman, from Manhattan not New Jersey. She was well educated, literary even, and hers was the only other black household I had ever visited with shelves of books in it. Sam was a quiet, strong, dark-skinned boy, with beautiful hazel eyes that had flecks of green in them. He was far more interested in riding bikes and deejaying than in reading, but books were a familiar sight to him and he didn't think they were dangerous like everyone else around us did. Sam and I were close, but he was something of a loner. He didn't much care for team sports or for the other boys I hung around with, and that put limits on the amount of time we spent together.

When I wasn't with Sam, I split my time between the basketball courts at the park and friends' homes on the black sides of Fanwood and Scotch Plains. I became tight with one of Sam's classmates, a boy named Antwan who lived a ten-minute walk from my house. Ant, as we called him, was handsome and well groomed, with ebony skin, a low-cut Caesar hairdo, and deep, brushed-out 360 waves, which he kept "spinning" beneath a black cut-off Calvin Klein stocking cap. He spent hours each day on the bench press fine-tuning his enviably muscular build. At fifteen, in Polo jeans, Timberland boots, and a white wife-beater tank top, he drew comparisons to Tyson Beckford, the male model with the Apollonian physique.

By age seventeen, Ant's torso was covered in tattoos like Tyson's, but it was Tupac Shakur who was his inspiration. "I wanna get that THUG LIFE tat across my stomach like Pac," he used to say as we idled away hours at the park or on his front porch, shooting baskets and the breeze. On his pumped-up right biceps there was the image of two emerald-hued hands clasped in prayer, framed in negative-relief against a burst of light, with Tupac's famous dictum—ONLY GOD CAN JUDGE ME—inscribed below in an intricate Old English font. On his left, there was a portrait of his newborn baby sister. One forearm spelled-out A-N-T in block letters; the other inner-arm displayed a page from the Old Testament turned to Psalm 23: "Even though I walk through the valley of the shadow of death, I will fear no evil . . ." I don't know whether Ant was religious or not; the ink seemed more about being *chic*, and Psalm 23 especially, because it spoke to our generation's paranoid sense of oppression and persecution, of being in foreign territory surrounded by enemies yet anointed and special, had become a smart fashion accessory.

Sometimes Antwan would come over to my house to work out in the basement when Charles and I were finished studying. The three of us clicked, and from time to time we would go together to Sayreville for teen night at Club Abyss. Abyss was like a parent's worst nightmare on teen night. Fifteen-, sixteen-, and seventeen-year-old black, white, and what people who have never been to Spain call "Spanish" girls came there less to dance than to simulate sex to a hip-hop beat. As a black dude, if you could just look and sound like enough of a thug, you could approach one of them and do it, too. I spent hours in the mirror before we went, getting my pose just right.

Charles, who was a kind of virtuoso of teen night, didn't need any practice. He had what Ant called "the gift" and pulled a variety of females like a hamstring, without trying. Ant and I didn't have the gift, but we did have our types and we zeroed in on them accordingly. For Ant, there was nothing better than a girl with lighter skin and straighter hair than his own. By far the darkest one in the trio, he strictly approached white or Latina chicks, avoiding girls that resembled him as though he hated them. (In this way, and in this way alone, he was willing to break with the School of Pac.) I couldn't understand Ant's mind-set in any way, but I had met enough black guys with it to know it was not unusual. My attitude toward women, on the other hand, was a lot more like Henry Ford's toward automobiles: Give me any color so long as it's black. Ant and I used to argue about this all day. In the end, though, he would say, and Charles would agree, that it really didn't matter what type of ho you preferred—playing women was a hobby, and the bottom line was that each was as disposable and interchangeable as the next.

I had just gotten my permit and was whipping down the street toward home one hot summer afternoon. The windows were down and Tupac's "Picture Me Rollin'" pumped from the speakers. Out of the corner of my eye, I peeped a shirtless Antwan beating a hasty path down the side of the road, his black do-rag like a pirate flag in the wind, his tattoos glistening beneath beads of sweat. As I pulled over to the shoulder, honking, he jogged up to the car and hopped in.

"Nigga, that's good timing!" he panted.

"What the hell are you doing on the side of the road without a shirt?" I teased.

"This white bitch I'm tossing up was supposed to give me some sneaker paper, but she ain't have my money, and we got into it," he explained. "Then her pops pulled up and I had to dip up out that winnnndooooow, nigg-uuuhhhhh! I barely got my shoes on." (Ant had this hilarious way of speaking in undulating tones, drawing out certain syllables in the words he chose to stress; had he been born twenty years earlier he'd have been a soul singer or soapbox preacher for sure.) We both started cracking up.

In some far-off region of my mind I knew the way that Ant treated girls was wrong. But it didn't strike me as particularly bizarre. All of my friends who could do it, me included, got money out of bitches and professed to look down on them in the process. We called this "running game." The better you could run or spit game, the more respect you could get from your boys. I sported a $1,500 gold chain on top of $500 hand-knit Coogi sweaters from Australia, which my girlfriend, Stacey, bought for me with cash.

My relationship with Stacey was in many ways the fulcrum upon which I hoisted up my sense of self. A year younger than me, she was the epitome of the black girl I had hoped to attract when I chose Union Catholic over Delbarton that day in the car with Pappy. Winning her attentions authenticated my blackness and justified my swagger. Stacey was sassy and flip, flashy like a pinky ring. She modeled when she could, appeared in black magazines like *Hype Hair* and local fashion shows and beauty pageants. She rolled her plaid skirt three times at the waist and wore her cotton blouse open a button lower than it should have been. I was by no means the only one who coveted Stacey, and this, for me, only magnified her allure. I treated the clothes and jewelry that she bought for me like trophies, advertisements for my prowess.

They were also body armor, defense against the lingering gossip. People always talked about the way Stacey got her money, what drug dealers she ran around with on the side—girls run game, too. I didn't like to think about that; I couldn't let myself think about that. The point here, I knew enough to know, was not whether you had a solid relationship, whether you were equipped to treat other people with respect—most of us were not. The point was whether you were getting over—whether you were getting something out of the exchange. You certainly didn't *care* about the girl.

Money, hoes, and clothes, that's all a brother knows; Fuck bitches, get money; Gs up, hoes down; All I've got for hoes is hard dick and bubble gum—this was the rhetoric that was drummed (literally) into our heads. It wasn't the way my father felt about my mother. But Jay-Z told us straight up: We don't love these hoes. Not if we're going to be cool by his book. And on these matters we listened to him and those like him. If for some reason you did end up caring, as I hopelessly cared for Stacey, well, that was something to be kept close to the chest. You got no respect—not even from the girls themselves—for wearing your feelings on your sleeve. We called the me-myself-and-I position that we adhered to many things; most commonly we called it pimpin'.

I tried my best to keep it pimpin' in all matters concerning Stacey. There were so many rumors floating around about her. An especially resilient one was that a boy in her class named Marion had slept with her. She denied it. It was not improbable, though; we were all players and pimps, nasty girls and freaks in our own minds. I tried to brush it off until one morning a classmate handed me a tennis ball container's worth of carefully folded loose-leaf correspondence between Stacey and Marion. It spanned an entire year. My first response to the letters was not what it might have been. I didn't break things off with Stacey or even acknowledge Marion. Rather, I went into full-on damage-control mode like a one-man public relations firm, seeking to protect my reputation by any means necessary, to release a calibrated statement, to let everyone know I had my ho in check. I stormed through the sophomore corridor on a warpath. I found Stacey standing at her locker with a group of girlfriends and confronted her.

"What the fuck are these?" I screamed.

"Nigga, I don't know—what the fuck do they look like?" she casually replied, rolling her eyes and resuming the conversation with her friends as though I were not there. It was the final provocation that I needed. It felt as if my body were functioning on autopilot. What I knew I had to do and what I knew I would do became one and the same. The crowds of other students in the hallway suddenly seemed to vanish and all the noise of their chatter went mute. It was just Stacey and me standing there, as far as I was concerned, and all I could hear was a chopped-and-screwed mishmash of hip-hop aphorisms playing through my head, telling me in metered rhyme exactly how to treat a bitch, how to reach a bitch, who thinks she's all that: *Bitch get out of line? Slap her; Punch that bitch, slap that ho . . . All you heard was Poppa don't hit me no' mo'!*

I yanked Stacey by the arm and dragged her kicking and screaming out of the building, her friends staring in amazement. We marched through the parking lot and into the woods that surrounded a park down the street from the school. As soon as we were alone and before she could say a word, I brought the back of my hand down across the side of her cheek in one swift motion that would land her in the nurse's office. The sound reverberated off the trees with a sickening *thwack*. It sounded like an isolated high-hat from one of Puffy's drum machines. I threw the canister of notes at her head and lunged for her feet, trying to rip off the sneakers I had bought for her for Christmas that year. She grabbed my shoulder for balance and our eyes met. Her mascara ran, dissolving the steel veneer on her face as she whispered, "Thomas, Thomas, please stop."

I felt myself suddenly emerge out of autopilot. I had been delusional with rage, envisioning myself some affronted suburban Iceberg Slim, but it was hard as hell to keep the act going now. Looking at her, at the fear and hurt in her eyes, the fear and hurt that I had put into her eyes, I no longer felt ice-cold. I wasn't pimpin'. I felt nauseated. More than anything, I felt terribly sorry. We both crumpled to the ground, huddled in each other's arms, sobbing.

As we slowly made our way out of the woods and back toward school, I glimpsed my brother's aquamarine Camaro fly by. "There they are!" I heard him shout, as he broke to the shoulder. It was a warm day, and the T-tops were in the trunk. Clarence put the car in park, hopped through the open roof, and ran across the street to where we stood. As I feared, I could see Pappy in the passenger seat, waiting. "Hey, Stacey," Clarence said, nodding and lighting a cigarette. As scared as I was to see Pappy right then, I was equally grateful that my brother had come along for the ride. Clarence, in terms of disposition, was the polar opposite of our father. Whereas

Pappy treated everything as a matter of life and death and sought to prevent even the minutest problems from ever arising, Clarence's theory of life was more like: Hey, shit happens. He accepted that premise as a given and didn't ask many questions or judge anyone else's motives or mistakes. In that way he was the yin to my yang, too, and he was far more generous with his view of me and my behavior than I was with him.

Just a few weeks earlier, he had rescued me from a situation with Stacey that could have gone terrifically wrong. It was a holiday from school and I had taken the train to her aunt's house to see her. To my horror, mid-coitus, I contorted my leg into an awkward position; my knee slid out of place, locked up, and remained bent at a neat right angle, suspended in the air. I couldn't walk. Stacey's aunt, a police officer who carried a loaded strap and did not appreciate boys even talking to her niece, was due home in no time. As we scrambled to get me dressed, I called Clarence in a delirium. "I'll be there in ten minutes," he said, chuckling. "Just be ready when I pull up."

I thanked him profusely, and with Stacey's aid, hopped on my good foot over to the park across the street, where I lay down in a field and waited for my brother's sweet chariot to come and steal me away. A few moments later, from out of a marigold sandstorm I saw Clarence's Camaro shoot across the baseball fields toward me. He spotted his baby brother lying prostrate in the grass, an upside-down Air Jordan perched atop a beige chicken leg sticking up from the ground like a flagstick on a golf course. He punched the brakes, fishtailing the back of the car like he was Axel Foley in *Beverly Hills Cop*. Without cutting the ignition, he jogged over to me, picked me up gently, and dropped me through the open roof into the back-seat. We exchanged a quick pound, then he slammed the gas, hit off one more peel-out, and sped over the curb onto the street.

"Yo, thank you so much, Clarence!" I said once we were at a safe distance and I had caught my breath.

"Don't mention it, man," he said, lighting a cigarette in the dash-board and shrugging. "I've been looking for an excuse to take this thing out on the grass for a while now."

That was my brother, and I loved him. He wouldn't be able to save me this time, though—I knew that. When neither Stacey nor I had shown up to homeroom in the morning, the front office called Pappy at home, Clarence explained. Pappy, of course, had been waiting for that call all along.

When we got back to school, a shaken Stacey went inside to the nurse's office, where she claimed to have had a panic attack. Outside, Pappy wanted a word with me, he said. I braced myself for the deluge, but it didn't come. Very calmly he turned around in his seat.

"You know, Thomas, I never had a father growing up, so I'm learning how to be one as I go. That's the best I can do. You know that, right?"

"Yeah, Babe, I know that," I said.

"Well, let me just ask you something, then, son, because I really don't have the answer."

"Uh-huh."

"If you had spent years of your life trying to do something, son, trying to rear a thoroughbred, say, a thoroughbred who would go on to run beautiful races and make you proud, if you had sacrificed everything for this thoroughbred, giving it everything you could, giving it the best you had to offer, if you hoped that this thoroughbred would represent the best that you and your people could achieve—well, after all this effort, after all this time and hard work and hope, after all that, would you be able to just sit back and let your thoroughbred run around in the mud with a herd of mules and donkeys? I mean, it might get hurt doing that, right? It might really get hurt. Or—and this would be even worse, in my opinion—it might somehow start to believe that it, too, was a donkey or a mule. Now, that would be tragic, wouldn't it?"

I just stared; there was not much I could say. Clarence leaned out of the window, dragging on a cigarette. Classmates going to their cars for lunch pretended not to look.

"Well, I know you can't just keep that thoroughbred locked away forever," Pappy said, shaking his head slowly. "That ain't very realistic, is it, to keep it locked away?"

I went back into the building. I didn't feel like much of a thoroughbred right then, that was for sure. As for Stacey and her mysteriously welted cheek, she took an ice pack for the swelling and that was the end of it. No matter how many ways they put the question to her, she wouldn't snitch on me. For my part, I was a student of Biggie Smalls: I did not discuss my problems with my wife. I wouldn't talk about what had happened to anyone other than Charles; other students could speculate and make their own assessments. The result was that Stacey and I stayed together, people continued to gossip, Pappy continued to listen for the sound of me falling, and the very next week I came to school with a fresh new pair of Versace shades courtesy of my girlfriend.

In addition to my tabloidlike romantic life, I built up my reputation and stores of self-esteem at Union Catholic through my status as a basketball player. I was the starting point guard on the varsity team as a sophomore, beating out pissed-off juniors and seniors for the slot, and I grew haughty over the fact. I took it for a given that I would continue to improve and go on to play college ball. The game came easily to me, as it always had, and it seemed as if everything would simply fall into place.

One night at practice, Coach told me I wasn't getting my hands dirty enough on defense—that I was sitting back acting like a prima donna or something like that. By this time, I had developed a habit, along with Charles, of talking back to white teachers and authority figures at Union Catholic. The attitude was all Lil' Wayne: I do what I want, and you do what you can do about it. As a matter of reflex, I told Coach that he could take my defense and shove it. My teammates laughed. He went ballistic, face crimson, hurling abuse my way. I turned my back on him mid-tirade and walked out of the gym. Somehow, I thought that this would hurt him more than it would hurt me.

The next game on the schedule that week happened to be against Scotch Plains–Fanwood High School, against the kids I had grown up with and played with at the park since childhood. It was a game I had been waiting for all season. Besides the usual bragging rights, I had an unfriendly rivalry going with Scotch Plains's star, a boy named Larry, and we were both spoiling for a showdown. When I came out of the locker room and onto the court the afternoon of the game, there were a lot of familiar faces in the bleachers, including Ant's and Stacey's and Clarence's. I waved to them and started loosening up when Coach called me over to the sideline. I hadn't spoken to him since practice.

"What's up, Coach?"

"What's up is that you're coming off the bench today."

"What? But Coach, this is my hometown. That's embarrassing!"

"I know," he said. "And that's the point."

I played less than five minutes that game, while Larry dropped more than twenty points and laughed at me from the court. Scotch Plains won by double digits. I went home in a terrible funk. Pappy, who never could acclimate himself to the idea of a white man dressing down a black boy in public, whatever the reason, wasn't happy when he heard about it. He ordered me to quit and offered to transfer me from Union Catholic to a list of other schools, but to the surprise of us both, I balked at this deal, at the thought of not being around Stacey every day. In this way, I was what Ant called "a terry cloth nigga"—*too* soft. I just couldn't do it. To my shame, I felt the need to stay put, to stay with Stacey at all costs. The truth is that, more than even playing basketball, it was being with Stacey, I felt, that validated me. I couldn't imagine losing that validation for anything. Instead of leaving, I decided to play AAU ball and go to summer camps, hoping that would be enough to get a scholarship to college, even though I knew it almost certainly would not.

One of the camps I attended the summer after quitting the team was run by Bob Hurley, the coach of St. Anthony High School in Jersey City, consistently one of the top-ranked teams in the nation. His was the only school for which I might have been willing to part with Stacey. The difference between the varsity squad at St. Anthony and the one at Union Catholic is the difference between

Paris, France, and Paris, Texas—they're not on the same map. All week long at camp I played hard, trying to shine in front of Coach Hurley, whose own son had famously made it to the NBA. I did well in league play, and when Pappy came to the rural campsite to pick me up he introduced himself to the renowned coach, who told him he had noticed me and that I was welcome to work out with his team, the Friars, when school resumed in the fall.

My mother drove me out to St. Anthony twice. What I remember most about the long trek there from Fanwood is the overwhelming stench that sets up shop in your nostrils as soon as you approach the Jersey City exit on the Turnpike. It smells like a little patch of Mexico City has been grafted onto the Garden State and you are waylaid in it. My mother and I rolled up the windows and turned off the highway, creeping through bleak service streets, looking for the gym, which, to our surprise, was smaller and of even more modest construction than the one I had used as a child at Holy Trinity. Inside, though, there was nothing modest about the game that was under way. I spotted Coach Hurley—besides my mother, the only Caucasian in the room—stalking the sidelines, tracking the action with the severest blue eyes in the world.

As I approached, he studied me for a second—piercing through me, it felt like. He was polite, neither friendly nor unfriendly; he greeted my mother and then smiled at me with his mouth but not those eyes. Get loose and link with the other boys on the sideline, who have next, he told me, and then his attention was no longer mine. That is the way a Don looks upon the face of a flunky, I thought and began to stretch. Two or three of the players in the gym I recognized from camp, the rest I hadn't seen before, and one of them I knew by reputation to be Anthony Perry, the star of the team (insofar as there are things like individual stars at a place like St. Anthony), a soon-to-be McDonald's All-American, and one of the best high school players in the country on anybody's list. His team won.

I stepped with my five onto the court and it occurred to me that I was the most conspicuously dressed player in the room, with my patent leather Air Jordans, black Nike socks and matching shorts and shirt—matching everything, Nike everything, from head to toe—and this made me self-conscious. The other boys mostly were dressed in old maroon-and-maize St. Anthony gear and the sneakers they'd been given, which made me think that clothes either were the last thing on their minds or a luxury they couldn't afford, or both. I was running in the off guard position now because the point guard of the team was on my squad. He was this short, thick, almost eggplant-black boy ("blurple" was Stacey's term for the color), with a squarish head. He reminded me of one of the scowling members of Full Force, those bullies Kid 'n Play were always fleeing from in the old *House Party* movies. The boy had declined to speak to me when I introduced myself to him, which didn't especially bother or surprise me; I figured he was just focused—everyone in this gym was so damn focused you got the impression that were they to apply similar effort to, say, the study of medicine, they'd find the cure for cancer or the secret to immortality.

On the first play of the game, my man, who I had inches on, took the ball directly at me, hard, leaned me on my heels, then stepped back for a mid-range jumper. He missed and I boxed him out for the rebound, which was coming directly at us. I assumed I would grab it over him with ease. I kind of half jumped for the ball and, anticipating myself, began to turn my attention toward the other basket and to offense. I had one hand on the ball when suddenly it began to lift itself up. In a flash, I saw the crotch of one of the forwards from the other squad in my face as he hammered the pill back through the net and swung from the rim. "Let's go!" he shouted, and sprinted back on defense, squatting at half-court to slap the ground. I went to get the ball and inbound it to the point guard, who was staring right through me.

"D the fuck up, nigga," he said as I trotted back behind him.

My team got run off the court that game. I managed to get through it without any egregious mistakes. I hit a jump shot, guarded the rock, didn't commit any turnovers. My man scored on me several times, which was a problem, but all in all I didn't feel so bad—you win some and you lose some. I sat down on the sideline thinking about what to do better next run but not displeased, when the point guard with the quadrilateral headpiece walked by. He was still breathing pretty hard, harder than I was. I looked up at him and he looked down at me, and just when I thought he was about to speak, he began to clear his throat, really clearing it out, from somewhere deep down in his esophagus or even deeper. He looked me in the eye and then he spat, emphatically, hawking what turned out to be the single largest gob of phlegm I have ever seen onto the floor beside me. It hit the wood almost with a splash and formed a kind of jiggling, glossy puddle there. What the fuck—does this guy have emphysema or something? I thought. Before I could register a reaction of any sort, though, he turned his back on me. This exchange (*exchange?* no, "exchange" is not the word—complete dismantling is more like it; I think my mother was in the stands) rattled me to the core. In one bold stroke, he had established his territory and annihilated my confidence, snapping that shit in two like a stalk of celery.

The second time I went to St. Anthony, a week or so later, was much easier simply because on a certain level I had stopped caring. I found myself on Perry's squad. At game point, I caught the ball at the top of the key, pump-faked, and drove past my man for a quick pull-up jump shot. In the air, I spotted Perry on the baseline drifting to the basket and dumped the ball down to him with both hands. He caught it and flipped it behind his head for an easy layup. Our team won. Perry pointed at me and nodded and a couple of players gave me dap as we headed to the sideline. One of them took me aside and said: "Yo, you had that shot, son; don't just look to pass, go for yours next time." I nodded and said I understood.

Sometime after I got back home I told Pappy that I didn't think I needed to go back to St. Anthony. He looked puzzled, but said that was fine—he had meant it when he told me that he didn't care to see another black athlete or entertainer. One thing he wanted to say, though, and something he wanted me to think hard about was what Coach Hurley had told him. "Thomas doesn't have the toughness," Hurley said. "He isn't from where my boys are from. I could tell that he was out of his element the moment he walked through the door, and so could my boys. My boys are hungry, and Thomas is not."

That assessment, as much as it stung, was fair. Though my comparative privilege embarrassed me, and I clung to the delusion that I could be just as hard as Hurley's boys if I tried, I knew deep down that I wasn't nearly as tough or as desperate. The truth is that I *wasn't* all that hungry for a life devoted to sports or entertainment when I really thought about it—and Pappy had made it plain from the beginning that I didn't have to be.

Like hip-hop, basketball had simply always been around me: You're black, and you'd better know how to hoop. I was better than average at it. But coming into such close contact with the life-and-death manner in which the boys at St. Anthony approached the game, the frenzied and terrified way they played basketball—a sport at the end of the day—the way they made this game their lives gave me real pause. Even I knew the disheartening math, even I knew that only one or two players—at generous maximum—from that undefeated St. Anthony squad, perhaps the best varsity boys' team in the whole country, would get a shot at a career in the NBA. And what becomes of the rest of them?

That was my junior year, what Pappy called the single most crucial phase of a high school student's life, the moment the SAT moves from abstraction to reality. How you do on this test, Pappy said, more than anything else you can do right now, will determine what kind of life you will be able to lead. I was still trying as hard as ever to keep it real and I continued to play AAU ball and to understand myself mostly through my body, but I also began to suspect that "going for mine" now would need to mean something more than taking open jump shots.

CHAPTER FOUR

Street Dreams (Who Am I to Disagree?)

People say that hip-hop is more than just a genre of music—it's a certain bounce in your stride, it's the way you shake hands, it's the ideas that circulate in your head. It's the ideas that don't circulate in your head. A philosopher might say it's a way of *being* in the world. An authority on the subject, like the rapper Nas, says, "It's that street shit, period."

As I exited my senior prom, it was one of Nas's songs, a track titled "Street Dreams" that rattled out of the trunk of my friend's new chrome-rimmed Acura RL, filling the banquet hall's parking lot with a thugged-out adaptation of the Eurythmics classic. That night, in a monsoon wave of Fahrenheit cologne, Cuban-link gold chains, freshly braided cornrows, gravity-defying hair weaves, pastel-colored tuxedos, gator boots, painted-on evening gowns, and six-inch stilettos, several dozen African-American members of the Union Catholic Regional High School class of 1999 hopped into a cavalcade of rented Range Rovers, Mercedes-Benzes, Cadillacs, and BMWs and sped down the Garden State Parkway to a seedy and unassuming strip of beachfront motels in the Seaside Heights section of the Jersey Shore.

There, far from any chaperone's probing eye, I found myself sprawled in a smoke-filled box of a hotel suite, passing back and forth bottles of Hennessy and passionfruit Alizé. Between hot sips of cognac, I could make out classmates gutting Dutch Masters cigars and filling the brown paper shells back up with sticky mounds of Chocolate Thai. Eyelids narrowed into slits as orange-tipped blunts lit the darkness like fireflies on a still summer night. Biggie Smalls's baritone vocals bumped from the stereo, punctuating the charged silence, his lyrics virtually begging us to see life his way: *"The williest/Bitches be the silliest/The more I smoke, the smaller the Phillie gets."* The sex, like violence, erupted fast and without warning: Kids broke off into twos—and threes—keeping time to some secret rhythm as the beds turned into one big horizontal dance floor. We were enacting scenes straight out of our favorite rap songs: *"Tell your friends to get with my friends and we could be friends, shit we could do this every weekend,"* Puff Daddy boasted on "Big Poppa," Biggie's paean to group sex, weed-smoking, and general thug living. That was the theme song for our weekend; those guys were our role models. We knew these songs by heart. Stealing glimpses of myself in the mirror was like watching late-night Black Entertainment Television—Medusa-faced Versace sunglasses glaring at me; a gold Jesus-piece medallion swinging back and forth across my chest like a tetherball; and a faceless, honey-toned piece of flesh bouncing up and down, *in flagrante*. It was, as the saying goes, all good.

Night had dissolved into early afternoon when I awoke. Takira—in whose arms I was almost certain I had fallen asleep—was no longer lying next to me. The room stank and was deserted except for Charles, who sat at the table in the far corner, smoking a Newport Light and talking to his friend Nate in herky-jerky gestures and rapid-fire sentences.

"Word is born, yo, I had Latitia like: 'What's my name, what's my name!'" he cried, pantomiming the act, grinning wildly. "I think I left her pigeon-toed!" His words trailed off into hiccupping laughter.

Nate, who doled out emotional cues like a miser hands out C-notes, made an expression that could have been interpreted to mean just about anything. "Yeah, I had my way with Candy, too," he said, his face disappearing behind a plume of minty smoke.

The three of us got dressed and went upstairs to the room where our female classmates were staying. After a couple knocks, the door, its paint peeling in off-white sheets the size of an open fist, swung open to reveal Candy in a Union Catholic phys ed T-shirt and silk headscarf, her bare thighs the color of mahogany. I could see Takira and Latitia in the background, lounging on the two beds. Last night was no dream. We waddled into the room, busting sags so low that with one false step our pants would fall around our ankles. I was hitching size 36 jeans onto a twenty-eight-inch waist. The girls' room looked like a scale model of Tupac's mythical Thug's Paradise: There were half-naked bitches with full black asses prancing around, ashtrays heaping with stubbed-out blunts, discarded fast food wrappers, empty liquor bottles, and, with our presence, a trio of niggas with attitude to spare and deep pockets full of condoms.

Without missing a beat, Nate produced a flask-sized bottle of Hennessy from his hoodie, which either was half-full or half-empty depending on how you looked at it. He swigged on the thing like it was a Nantucket Nectar. Charles grabbed the remote control, flipping between a Lakers game and music videos on BET. I sank into Latitia's bed and let the alternating images of the young, black, and famous stream from the TV and trickle into my head. Fighting down Nate's cognac with a fruity cupful of Alizé, I heard Takira whisper in my ear, her breath a noxious perfume of weed and Frosted Flakes: We can do anything we want, she told me, wearing only her red Victoria's Secret underwear and an open bathrobe. The proposition repulsed me. In school, I never liked Takira, the B.I.G. mourner, but the previous night we had somehow become lovers. What am I doing here? I thought to myself. Right then I wanted nothing so much as just to be at home, eating my mother's bacon and eggs, feeling calm or perhaps just bored, watching the Lakers game with my father or shooting baskets in the driveway. I brushed Takira off with a lame excuse as I felt Latitia's leg move on top of mine beneath the bedspread. "Do you want to go down to your room?" she asked. I forgot about going home.

Besides the obvious, there was an additional draw to getting with Latitia: She was Marion's girlfriend. Just a few weeks earlier, I had been in the cafeteria with Charles, complaining over a lunch of

French fries and chocolate milk that the Marion thing just wouldn't go away; that word about him and Stacey was rampant, spreading like an ink stain or a disease, even though I had made a show of parading around in the $400 silk shirt she had bought me as a sign of solidarity. "Fuck the Versace, nigga, you gotta step to him!" Charles said. "No matter what, you can't ever let anyone disrespect."

Charles meant what he said. I knew that. He was one of those guys who, if he were to get mugged at gunpoint for his wallet, would say "fuck you" to the gunman and get shot putting up a fight. Not because he gave a damn about the wallet or anything like that, but because he couldn't stand the humiliation of it all. Death (or at least a vigorous ass-whooping) before dishonor was his modus operandi. Tupac was real, Charles once told me, for taking five shots in the attempted robbery that nearly killed him. "They took his Rolex anyway," I said. "That's beside the point," Charles said. "Pac stood his ground, which is what mattered."

"True," I said, and on a certain level I agreed with him—that *was* what mattered.

Still, on another level it was getting stupider and stupider for me to try to stand my own ground whenever it was contested. I posted some of the highest SAT and SAT II scores in the school that year, and Pappy explained to me that I could go places with them. Before that, I had only conceived of college in terms of the men's basketball rankings. Now all of a sudden, off the team and having done better than I ever imagined on standardized tests, I found myself putting together applications to fifteen of the best academic institutions in the country. Most eighteen-year-olds with ambitions of going where Pappy had shown me to apply would do anything in their power to avoid a fistfight.

Talking the matter over with Charles, though, it became clear that I would not be able to be like most of those other eighteen-year-olds. I was going to have to step to Marion, and that was that. However foolish it was and despite his own college dreams, Charles would back me up, too. He would back me up whether it was one-on-one or the two of us on twenty. Charles was loyal to a fault. But what dumbfounded him to no end, what pained him—his face looked like he had sipped rancid milk—was that I had even put myself in such a position in the first place, that I had let myself get so close to Stacey. "This should never happen over a bitch," he said, shaking his head. All my boys echoed this sentiment at one time or another: Never trust a bitch; never love a bitch. Those were the rules, and they were beyond questioning. Why I couldn't just live by them was a mystery to us all.

The afternoon of the lunchroom chat, I boarded Marion's Irvington-bound bus with Charles in tow, my gold chain wrapped tightly around my fist, my back, so to speak, against the wall. We took our seats in the rear and when the driver pulled into the street I stood up, walked forward and smashed my chain, and the medallion attached to it, into Marion's jaw. Latitia screamed, but Charles made sure that no one broke us up. "Nigga, I've been dying for this," Marion snarled. At well over six feet, he was a lithe kid who looked like a young Jay-Z with more refined features. He fought his way into a standing position and out into the aisle. Our classmates moved away, parting to both sides like the curtains in a theater. This seemed appropriate, we were on stage now, and I wanted everyone to see.

The bus driver slammed his brakes—which sent us flying forward, holding on to each other for stability with one hand while railing on each other with the free one—before making a beeline back to school and radioing in for help. The two of us spilled from the bus into the parking lot, partners in a furious tango, pausing to kick off our unlaced Wallabees so they wouldn't get scuffed, then lunging at each other like skinny, demented pit bulls. Our classmates hung from the windows, pumping their fists, roaring their approval. I knew how to box a little bit. Pappy, a man who even in old age could handle himself with his hands, had taught me the basics when I was a kid: how to bob and weave, parry a punch, take a punch. But this was not boxing, there was no grace to this, no artistry—Marion and I were swinging for the fences on each other's faces, dodging nothing, eating each other's knuckles in lumpy bites.

Outside, everything began to move in delirious slow motion. I saw my fist crawl past Marion's nose, missing the mark by inches. I saw his lanky arm cock back and felt my own nose grow hot. I felt my eyes get wet and blurred. I saw my fist connect with Marion's chest. I saw Marion lose his footing and fall backward. I saw myself on top of his ass in the bushes edging the walk. I saw him on his knees. I saw my fist come down on his head one, two, three, four times like a hammer beating a stubborn nail into submission. The damn nail would not submit. It felt like one of those nightmares where no matter how hard you swing, the decisive blow eludes you and your tormentor continues to taunt, undeterred. I kept trying to knock him out, no longer able to hear my classmates' cheers or see anything beyond Marion's close-cropped head in my hands. I didn't see myself go down. I felt my right shoulder pop loose from its socket before I saw my vice principal's flushed cheeks and terrified gaze hovering over me. I felt myself pinned to cement. I felt the pain in my nose, my eyes, my arm, my back, my bloodied feet—it hit me from both sides, top to bottom, like a supercollider.

Even though there were rules on the books against fighting, I didn't get suspended for this, partly because I was, compared to my peers, a much more promising student and partly because my father just gave more of a damn than most. At the faintest whiff of trouble concerning his boys, Pappy would sweep into the school's administrative offices with the severity of a man from another era, decked out in his finest worsted suit and tie, hair pomaded back, tortoiseshell glasses magnifying his gaze, wing tips shined to a mirror polish, and demand to speak with the principal. "The principal may be busy," he would tell the nervous secretary whose unfortunate job it was to run interference, "but he's going to have to come out and see me."

If on the occasion Clarence or I had done wrong, Pappy would not defend us or object to punishment, but there was nothing the school could do that would approach what awaited us at home. He made this so clear to all of us that there were times when the same teachers who had called him in reversed themselves and lobbied for clemency on our behalf. Pappy's point in these instances, then, was not to secure special treatment for his children. The point was that if the white administrators of the school were going to discipline his boys, his black boys, its head would have to justify this decision to Pappy's satisfaction—and also he would have to know that he would have to do so every single time. But Pappy didn't scream or shout; he argued—forcefully, rationally, carefully, and with an intellectual sophistication that was uncommon at the schools Clarence and I attended. With his gold Phi Kappa Phi tie bar and with his deep Texan voice, he was intensely formal and formidably intense. Everyone knew Dr. Williams at Union Catholic, and they dreaded an altercation with him.

"It sounds to me like this is a case of unrequited lust and that Thomas has been provoked by a would-be Lothario," Pappy insisted. "My son isn't going to be punished for defending himself against a bully." I sat there in silence. The truth is I had spared my father some of the less flattering details when presenting my side of the story. The principal and the vice principal—whose tackle I could still feel—were the kind of ethnic white men who had seen it all, racking up decades between them in the New Jersey interparochial school system. Each looked quizzically at the other and then with sympathy at Pappy. They had nothing but respect for my father, and they wanted to make that clear. It would be a shame, they said, for something like this to compromise my college applications, which was why they were going to be lenient this time. Without going into any particulars, however, what they both wanted to know was why a nice kid like me with such a nice family would be running around with a girl like *Stacey* in the first place. Didn't I know that she was trouble? Didn't my father know this? The split-second wince on Pappy's face hurt much more than Stacey's infidelity had.

I knew that my courtship of Stacey was an open, festering wound for Pappy, a source of lasting embarrassment against which he could not defend himself. Like Charles, honor meant everything to Pappy, though he had different ideas of what that word signified. Pappy couldn't give a damn about a street rep. He was self-schooled—a black, self-described bastard from the segregated South who had taught himself how to live from the beat-up copies of Plato's *Dialogues* and *Aesop's Fables* he'd managed to dig up in the meager colored library in Fort Worth and at the little Jewish synagogue in Galveston, where a stunned rabbi had invited him to study after Pappy had won a blind-entry essay competition with a piece on Maimonides.

All Pappy ever wanted to do in life was to distinguish himself, to be a man capable of commanding respect in a world that was madly hostile to anyone who looked like him. A world as unrecognizable to Charles and me as ours was to him. Pappy's word was his bond and his name was all he had, all that he could control. He didn't keep it real; he kept his name out of the street. I had brought shame home with Stacey. I was continuing to bring shame home, for he knew I had no intention of distancing myself from her and, powerful as he was, short of moving the family back across the country, he was powerless to keep me away from her.

For Pappy, it was all very simple. If life in fact was a chess game and I had taken Stacey as my queen, well, then my king was terrifically compromised. At best she was pure foolishness in his eyes, a street chick, five minutes with her amounted to a terrible price to pay for a piece of ass. At worst, there was the prospect of pregnancy, whether by me or by someone else—the difference was negligible to him and the potential for disaster incalculable. It kept him up at night. But Pappy and I saw the world through different lenses: What he found so troubling I found intoxicating—Stacey *was* street and that was what was so hot. She was 'hood, she was hip-hop, she was black, she was *real*. She had my nose open, Pappy told me. He was right.

————

I was propelled into bed with Latitia by the winds of my ego and by my hatred for Marion. Inside the motel room, however, with just the two of us together, my desire to keep it real, my thirst for revenge against Marion, it all faded away, receding like the ocean tide outside the crusted window. As her clothes piled up into a lace-capped mound on the floor, I noticed, as if for the first time, just how pretty Latitia was. With soft, wavy hair, sun-kissed caramel skin, and a body shaped more like a teardrop than an hourglass, she could have been a Brazilian exchange student or one of Gauguin's Tahitian nudes. I reminded myself that I'd had a crush on her since I was fourteen years old. I let myself get lost in her embrace and in the moment, forgetting about trying to be hard or *gangsta* or disrespectful. For a minute, I forgot that she was a bitch.

Suddenly there was a violent rapping at the door. I tried to ignore it, but it only grew louder. "Fuck, who is it?" I said.

"Nigga, it's Charles, open up!"

Latitia hopped under the covers as I threw on some basketball shorts and cracked the door. There was Charles holding Candy by the hand.

"I'm sorry, yo, but Nate and Takira locked us out; this is the only place we can go," he said. I either stared at him or shrugged or laughed, I can't remember which, but I know I didn't resist. What could I have said—that I was feeling tender toward Latitia and that now was not a good time to interrupt, that we had emotionally connected just now? Charles barged in. "Don't worry, nigga, you won't even know we're here," he said as Candy—who at seventeen *was* shaped like an hourglass and built thick like a 2 Live Crew

73

video dancer—met eyes with me, pursing her lips into a half-smile that landed in nebulous territory somewhere between babelike innocence and pure wickedness. I could have gladly bounced right then from the room, from the Shore, from the world, and I think Latitia could have, too, had things been different. But she said, "Fuck it, it's cool," which surprised me, and I realized that I would have to stay. After all, what would it make me look like if I left? It would make me look like I had caught feelings over a bitch. It would make me look corny as hell.

"No doubt," I said, and I slunk back over to Latitia.

Now and again I glanced over at the adjacent bed (I couldn't help it). Charles was pure business, focused, like he was about to beat a video game. Candy was wailing at the top of her lungs, saying she'd always wanted this, which even then struck me as one of the most preposterous declarations I had ever heard. I looked back down at Latitia, who had closed her eyes, perhaps also her ears. If any of this made Charles the least bit uncomfortable, he was able to conceal it.

I couldn't take it. Latitia and I went into the bathroom to take a shower. When we returned, Charles had lit a cigarette and put Biggie's "One More Chance" on the portable CD player. I flopped onto the bed with Latitia and tried to crack some jokes when Candy, visibly tipsy, got up and stumbled toward us, collapsing on top of me. She lay there, motionless, as Biggie slow-flowed about prophylactics and being "black and ugly as ever." I watched Latitia get up and walk away as Candy started to kiss my neck. There were things that I had wanted to say to Latitia, I realized, things that I now knew would go unsaid. I looked over to the other bed and saw

Charles on top of her; she was giggling, and I knew right then that I was powerless to treat her like anything other than a silly ho.

I wouldn't have been able to put it into words at the time, but the truth is that we had got caught up in one great big demeaning dance, all of us: Marion, Charles, Stacey, me, Latitia, Takira, Candy . . . , you could go on down the line. We all had memorized the steps to this number early on—and sometimes it was the girls who took the lead. A wave of sadness waxed over me then waned as quickly as it came. Candy had taken off her shirt and was telling me that she'd always wanted this.

Without fully realizing it, however, I already had begun the long process of unlearning the routine. At the very end of the school year, when a classmate, Jerry, who had felt provoked over some slight he thought I had given him—or maybe it was a slight I really had given him, the difference in these situations is semantic— challenged me (and Charles, indirectly) to an after-school fight that coming Friday, Charles started making arrangements to meet him. But I could find no good reason to fight Jerry, to want to fight Jerry, to waste my time dealing with Jerry, aside from that all-purpose issue of "respect," of course.

"He's disrespecting," Charles said. Who cares about Jerry's respect? I thought to myself. It was clear that this guy—a quick-tempered seller and user of drugs—was one step from getting stuffed away in one of those high schools for kids with emotional and behavioral disorders, two steps from jail, and uncountable steps removed from anything like a shot at a good college. Who cared what he thought—screw what he thought, I wanted to say, wanted to shout until I was hoarse—but "word up" was all I could muster.

Without the SATs to prepare for, Charles was no longer coming home with me every day after school. Most days it was just Pappy and me, sitting in his study, half-listening to Jenny Jones or Ricki Lake, playing chess and talking until my mother got home from work. We would play every day. Pappy always played black, which moves second and is therefore a perpetual step behind white, always on the defensive, like the receiving side in tennis. And just like in tennis, when good players play chess, it is assumed that the receiving side, the side to go second, will lose. Like breaking serve, a win or a draw for black is considered an upset.

"Why do you always want to be black?" I often asked him. "Don't you want to go first?"

His response never changed. "I prefer black because it's a realer representation of life, son," he would say. And he would add: "The odds are stacked against you when you go second, which requires you to play smarter—you've got to think."

Born left-handed, Pappy painstakingly taught himself as a child to write with his right hand and as a result it became the stronger of the two. The same way he had learned penmanship with his off hand, Pappy had made himself an even stronger chess player with black than with white. Most games, he beat me handily.

The afternoon after Jerry's challenge, I couldn't concentrate on chess at all. I was playing sloppily and Pappy could tell that something was wrong. I debated with myself whether I should tell him about Jerry or not. I fiercely admired the fact that Pappy was no coward. He wasn't like a lot of the white fathers I had known at

Holy Trinity; he wasn't meek or passive-aggressive, and he didn't think that fighting was inherently wrong or some sort of sin. If Pappy had a problem with you or you had one with him, he would address you to your face, like a man. He was old-school like that. Turning the other cheek is foolishness, he would say. As he saw it, there were times when the right thing to do—the ethically right thing to do—was to resort to violence. Malcolm X had a metaphor that resonated with Pappy: If you step on my foot, then you've just surrendered your right to tell me how I ought to get you off it. Pappy hated bullies. Bullies step on other people's feet. A coward accepts the affront; a man defends himself.

Finally I just came out with it and asked him what he thought I should do about Jerry. Leaning back in his worn leather swiveling-chair, in one of his colorful Nike jogging suits, he pulled at the coiled hairs of his salt-and-pepper beard, which seemed to grow a pinch saltier by the day, and pondered my question. "You should come home from school one period early on Friday," he said. "Just walk home instead of taking the bus."

This was not the answer I had necessarily expected, but it was one that I knew I could trust. He didn't lecture me that day as he might have and as I had expected. Maybe he could tell that I was going through some things and that now was not the time to apply any more pressure. Or maybe he figured that it was pointless, that I was eighteen and impetuous, and that he couldn't protect me from everything anymore. Or maybe he was just tired of it all, himself. I promised him that I would do as he told me.

That Friday was hell. Everyone was talking shit back and forth, calling their boys and their big brothers to come through, psyching themselves up like child soldiers drunk off blood in some war-ravaged African province. Jerry had been calling me a faggot and a bitch all around town, which by extension reflected on Charles, which by extension somehow reflected on Charles's neighborhood. And that was serious, because Charles's neighborhood did not produce any faggots or bitches, as far as he and his boys were concerned. Over the course of the week, things had metastasized from an infinitesimal problem between Jerry and me (and, of course, by extension Charles), to a meta-problem between Jerry's Linden/Rahway hometown and Charles's Piscataway/Plainfield neighborhood.

When I told him, Charles was deeply insulted that I was not going to show, but he stopped short of contradicting Pappy's advice.

"You shouldn't go either," I said, but that was an exercise in futility; his boys were on their way and Charles was going to go.

"I ain't a pussy," Charles replied. I shrugged and dapped him, telling him I understood, but I was going to do what my father had told me, and I'd see him later. As I walked out the side exit of the main building, bailing on Charles and his gathering crew, I knew I was making a decision that would carry real consequences. I knew that I was closing a door not only on Charles and Jerry and everyone else but on a part of myself, too.

When I got home, sweaty from the two-mile walk and the late-spring sun, Pappy, looking up from the paper, greeted me from his desk. Without mentioning what we both knew I had just avoided, he handed me three letters. I had been rejected by Stanford and admitted into Johns Hopkins and Georgetown on full-tuition academic scholarships.

I was beside myself. My brother had not gone to college and neither had any of his friends. Sometimes I overheard my father's white prep-school students talk about far-off places like Georgetown, but I didn't know anyone who looked like me—other than a handful of very tall and talented basketball players—who did that. I read the letters aloud. Pappy just stared at me with the hint of a smile curling up at the corners of his mouth. "You see?" he said when I had finished, then he returned to the *New York Times* spread out before him.

I was relieved and anxious at the same time. I went into my room, flopping onto the couch, the couch I sometimes snuck Stacey onto, and tried to imagine what college would be like. But I was unable to get Charles and Jerry out of my head. Like Tessie in "The Lottery," I had been caught up in all the little games and rituals of my village for so long that I had no idea what life outside was like. Unlike Tessie, I had decided I wanted to go away before it was too late. Now I didn't know what to expect. I turned on BET, cut the volume up all the way, and braced myself for the phone to start ringing.

CHAPTER FIVE

Slip the Yoke

Georgetown University sits on a manicured hilltop campus in Washington, D.C. In one direction it overlooks the Potomac River and Rosslyn, Virginia; in the other it opens onto the Northwest section of the capital, a residential area where preservation committees pulled a William F. Buckley Jr. maneuver, stood athwart history, and yelled Stop. The university grounds are covered with cherry blossom trees and dogwood, floral clusters, and heavy Flemish Romanesque architecture. Outside the main gates, the cobblestone streets are flanked with eighteenth- and nineteenth-century row houses and unattached mansions that come in pastels and boast prim lawns and price tags as long as telephone numbers. Madeleine Albright and John Kerry, John Edwards and the Kennedys—they all keep homes there. There are no Metro stops in Georgetown, a conspicuous fact that makes it a singularly difficult part of the city to get to or from without a car, and for which there are a variety of vague and contradictory explanations. The one told most often and convincingly is that the locals are trying to discourage the inward flow of out-of-town riffraff. Up and down M Street and Wisconsin Avenue, the neighborhood's two main thoroughfares, retail outlets of the Ralph Lauren and B&B Italia variety jostle for square footage. On the north side of campus, across from the university medical center, is the French embassy— so close, you can almost smell the smoke from the Gauloises. Day and night, schools of Porsches and Benzes swim beneath the trees and through the streets like German-engineered sharks. It is not uncommon to see a Bentley around. In the middle of one of the blackest metropolises in America—Chocolate City—Georgetown, the institution and the neighborhood, is an outpost of white and international privilege.

I arrived there in a backward New Era Yankees cap, Rocawear jeans as stiff as sheet metal, and a pair of brand-new yellow Timberland construction boots—all of which were worn in defiance of my new upscale environment and its sweltering heat. I brought with me stacks of Cash Money, Death Row, and Bad Boy albums, around twenty pairs of tennis shoes, a photo album's worth of pictures of Stacey, and something to prove. I imagined myself a kind of exiled representative of Union Catholic, of New Jersey, of hip-hop culture and blackness. When I settled into my room on the eighth floor of Harbin Hall, my white roommate's mother took one look at my closet and said: "Wow, it looks like Foot Locker in there!" I don't know why, but that made me feel proud. Pappy chuckled and said, "If only he'd worry about schoolwork as much as footwear."

My roommate, Bryan, and his family we all found friendly, which relieved my parents, but my mind was on another planet. I was missing Stacey, missing Charles; I didn't put much effort into getting to know the white kids I was meeting (or the Koreans, Europeans, Arabs, Haitians, or South Asians, for that matter). Which is only to say, I didn't pay attention to anyone not black. That was all I saw or was looking for. I felt alone and cocooned myself within the squiggled chalk lines of life as BET and Power 105 FM defined it for me.

My first weekend on campus, I found myself at a house party at a black apartment down on Prospect Street. The tenants of the house were four sophomores, some of whom ran track, and they had a big duplex in the Village A complex. I don't know whether I came with anyone or if I went there by myself, but I do know that I should have worn contact lenses. So much heat was being generated in there, my eyeglasses fogged as soon as I stepped inside. Bodies writhed and grinded up against the walls and one another (and even on top of the couches and on chairs) as Juvenile's "Back That Azz Up" blared. The only light came from the streetlamps beaming through the windows. In the shadows girls gave gratuitous lap dances and guys rolled up things to smoke.

I had never been to a college party before, let alone a black college party, and I was astounded that at a school ranked on the *U.S. News & World Report* top 25 list, I could stumble into a scene resembling so much what I had known at Union Catholic. I thought that my black classmates here would be all a bunch of Carlton Bankses and Stacey Dash characters from *Clueless*—privileged Oreos who would be wowed and intrigued by my studied 'hood persona. I thought that everyone would be busy cramming for biology. I thought that everyone would be in bed by ten. I thought that no one would listen to Cash Money Records. I was wrong on all counts. The 'hood, however besieged and dispersed, was alive and kicking at Georgetown. A curvy girl with molasses skin and short curly hair took me by the hand and let me dance with her. I leaned against the wall and pushed my belt buckle into her substantial gluteus maximus. Outkast's "Rosa Parks" came on and the whole floor shook as the party stomped and cried out in unison: *"Bulldoggin' hoes like them GEORGETOWN HOYAS!"*

The black world at Georgetown was only a microcosm of the wider black world outside the university gates, I discovered, but it was a world all the same, and one governed by its own rules and language, its own kings and queens, nobles and serfs. In many ways it was the negative of the surrounding white social order (a white order the likes of which I surely hadn't seen before): at the top of this obsidian pyramid were the students who remained closest to the street or on whom the scent of show business was most detectable. In roughly descending order this black Brahmin caste comprised: (a) the men's basketball team (especially those members who came from legitimate ghettos and who put the "athlete" in student-athlete), (b) the alpha females who hung out with, fought over, and fucked the men's basketball team, (c) the blossoming R&B singer Amerie and some of her friends (once it became clear she had a recording contract), (d) certain members of the football team (you can't name a single NFL player from Georgetown), (e) one or two members of the track team (track is almost never televised), and (f) the truly thugged-out non-athletes for whom affirmative action was either a godsend or a Sisyphean curse.

At the bottom of the heap were those—mostly males—who didn't rap or sing, who didn't walk and talk like they slung crack rock, who didn't have a wicked jump shot. Which is the same as saying, at the bottom of the pile were those of us who most resembled college students. I was terrified of winning such an ignoble fate. More than anything, I wanted to have some status; I wanted to be cool, which in turn led me to define myself in ludicrous opposition to the white world I was forced to move through. I became little more than a tourist in class and in my dormitory.

I was so frightened of the low status regular college guys enjoyed in the black community at Georgetown that I developed an antipathy for the classroom I hadn't even known in high school. I could count on one hand the number of microeconomics classes I attended during my first semester. One far from anomalous weekday morning, I found myself sitting in the cafeteria before class, eating breakfast, when I fell into a passionate conversation about gold chains with a guy from Philly.

"Why wasn't you rocking your chain at the club the other night, son?" he asked me.

"Because D.C. guys are wild," I said. "To be honest, I didn't want to risk getting it snatched."

"But nigga, that's the whole point! I *wish* a nigga would try and take my chain," he screamed. "I'm fiending to fight."

I didn't just miss that one morning econ class sitting there debating the wisdom of inviting an avoidable violent robbery. I ended up staying through lunch, dinner and, finally, even the late-night snack session. I bullshitted with successive waves of black diners—it was as if the cafeteria were my own personal drawing room—and missed an entire day's worth of school in the process. It didn't matter to me. The real drama of my new college life unfolded not in the classroom but in a handful of black friends' rooms, at the black bench in Red Square, and on the three or four designated black tabletops that cropped up at any given mealtime in the New South dining hall. These were little pockets of hip-hop reality within the larger white context, shriveled raisins afloat in vast seas of homogenized milk.

In addition to a masochistic attitude toward schoolwork, a closet full of very expensive clothes became both a necessity and a proxy for cool. I spent all of my spare money on gear and schemed on ways to get more. For every hour I spent at study, I squandered two worrying over my wardrobe. I was not alone or even that extreme in prioritizing things this way—I knew guys who put their clothes before even their personal health. My friend Maurice, a black boy from North Carolina on a scholarship, strutted onto the lawn one day after Thanksgiving break. He was dipped in costly layers of Iceberg apparel, brand-new Timberland boots, and a hefty Gucci link around his neck.

"Damn, that's fresh," I said. "How'd you get all that?"

"Yo, dawg, I be signing up for these medical experiments whenever I go home," he said.

"Medical experiments?"

"Dude, these Chapel Hill niggas'll give you like fifteen hundred a pop—I be volunteering for all types of shit!"

I was so isolated in this fiercely hierarchical black world, where the difference between being a winner and a loser often came down to the tag on your sweatpants; I was trying so hard to define myself as real and not to end up at the bottom of that status heap; I was so serious about all this, that what Maurice had told me that day did not immediately strike me as weird. In fact, I wondered if he might not be on to something. All I could think about was how to be cool.

For months I didn't even take the time to learn the names of the white kids I was living with. I gave them nicknames instead: the elegant, fey San Franciscan in the Helmut Lang pants, I called him Playboy; the neat Midwestern guy with the tousled red-brown hair, he became Rusty; Playboy's nondescript roommate from New Jersey, I called him Bruce, and when he dyed his hair blue I laughed and changed his name to Nigel. These white boys were not even like the fools my brother hung with back home. They were background décor, like all those silly-looking oil paintings hanging in Lauinger Library and Healy Hall—smug, smiling, self-satisfied faces that had nothing to do with my idea of interesting.

What was interesting, to me and to most of my black friends, was the promised land of Howard University. A half-hour bus ride away and a whole world apart, it was as close to the 'hood as college could get. At least once a week, I would leave Georgetown, take the G2 bus from Thirty-seventh and O Streets over to Bryant Street, and delve into the Real. Sometimes I went to get my hair cut. Other times I shopped for clothes or walked around aimlessly. It's not that I was unhappy or unthankful to be at Georgetown—on a certain level, I was aware that that was where I belonged. But on another less rational level I couldn't help but feel, when at Howard, like I was back in high school, staring at Jerome's Newark-bound bus pulling out of the parking lot—I wanted to get on.

The difference between Georgetown's black community and Howard's was not one of kind but of degree. The difference in degree, though, was titanic. Whereas at Georgetown there were a few scattered black girls holed up in Copley Hall or Village A, at Howard there was an entire Corbusian Radiant City of booty (booties stacked on top of booties on top of booties all the way into the sky!): an off-campus coed dormitory tellingly dubbed the Ebony Sex Palace. Brothers who weren't even college students drove from all over town and out of state just to post up outside the entryway and let their rims spin. Whereas at Georgetown you may have spotted Kofi Annan or Condoleezza Rice scuttling around campus in sober business suits, Howard was inundated with the likes of Fabolous Sport and DJ Clue, Jay-Z and DMX—'hood superstars who flossed platinum chains and diamond-encrusted Rolexes. Whereas at Georgetown you may have palmed a cold brew and marveled at the football team's stunning come-from-in-front defeat on homecoming day, at Howard, football was irrelevant; the only game in town was whatever you happened to be spitting at the girl standing in front of you at that moment in space-time.

Homecoming at Howard was a force of nature, not a sporting event. It was Freaknik, Carnival, NBA All-Star Weekend, the Puerto Rican Day Parade (minus the Puerto Ricans), Hot 97 Summer Jam, an ancient Incan mating ritual, and a mystic pilgrimage all rolled into one. It was an imaginary player's wet dream come true. Strutting around campus, ogling everything that moved, and trying with steely focus to obtain telephone numbers, I stumbled into one of Ant's boys from back home, a kid I recognized by face but not by name. We met eyes and he reached out to give me a pound. "Are you in school down here?" I asked. No, he wasn't in college, he told me, but he damn sure wasn't about to miss homecoming.

But it wasn't just a dormitory or one special weekend every year that made Howard so seductive—life in general was more extreme there. The area to the north and south of the McDonald's on Georgia Avenue bustled like a hip-hop Bois de Boulogne: *tout le monde* came out to get their promenade on. It was like real-life BET. Inside the gates, any day of the week the main quad provided a grand venue for a kind of performance art, transforming itself into an amphitheater for the choreographed reenactment of various Hype Williams music videos. Walking the yard, it felt as though if you put your mind to it, you could major in hip-hop studies, minor in the streets, and stick around to cop a PhD in pimpology— and to a certain extent you *could*.

Cats brought the 'hood with them to Howard in all sorts of different and inventive ways. At my friend Moe's dorm, one student ran a full-scale bodega out of his bedroom. He had a working cash register and a glass display case that he kept fully stocked; where his desk should have been was a cache of goods ranging from Tastykakes and Newport Lights to UTZ potato chips and refrigerated Mystic fruit juices and quarter waters. The only thing missing was a bright green Lotto machine. Out in the halls, kids from New York hustled drugs, stationing themselves by the elevators, slinging nickel and dime bags of smoke. Every week, some nineteen-year-old paid his way through school promoting a party or club night on the side. This was no longer the place where Thurgood Marshall studied law; this was the place where Sean Combs became Puff Daddy.

Traipsing those halls, the staccato rhythm of hip-hop, the unmistakable odor of game, the overwhelming sense of black cool met you at every turn, seeping from underneath every closed door and lilting from every open mouth. I used to get the same feeling going to Howard that I got on trips to Plainfield or Newark as a child: It was bad. You had the vague sense that you were doing something bad when you were there, and that could be exhilarating. I am sure there is still a serious side to Howard, but I did not see it. I saw brothers in turquoise chinchillas and head-to-toe interlocking Gucci logos. I saw a giant masquerade ball, a gangsta party where middle-class college kids—the sons and daughters of doctors and lawyers from suburban enclaves outside Atlanta and Chicago (north side)— as if just to prove that they were not middle-class, mingled and flirted with the street and everyone got dressed up as thugs and hustlers and hoes. And this vision corresponded neatly with the images I saw on television and in the D.C. clubs, with the way my friends got down back home in Jersey, with the way the faux-thugs and athletes carried themselves at Georgetown. This was *real*.

One night early in my first semester, as I was rifling through my closet, enveloping myself in a fog of Issey Miyake cologne, preparing to step with my friend Pup to catch the bus to Howard, my hallmate Rusty popped in my door and commented on my sweater in his nasally Midwestern monotone: "Rocking the Coogi, I see." He smiled. "I almost bought one at Neiman's once, but I looked more Bobby Huggins in it than B.I.G."

"Oh yeah?" I said, laughing—incredulous he knew what a Coogi was, that was how low my estimation was of these cats. "No shit, bro!" We bantered for a minute and I gave him a playful pat on the back and pushed past and out the door, not bothering to see what he was up to that night or to invite him out with me. It was a reflex reaction. Before that, I had never given a moment's consideration to Rusty—he was scenery. I would have assumed he felt the same about me. Pup and I continued on our way to Howard, but that night, once I had left, I remember thinking that it was kind of incredible that a white kid from Akron had got me, had reached out, had spoken my language and made me laugh—even if only on such a superficial level as a sweater. From then on Rusty and I began to talk when we passed each other in the halls and I found out that his name was John.

That first winter in Washington was difficult. I caught a cold that degenerated into a fever and, before long, a bronchial infection. It laid me out, wrapped in my leopard-print sheets sweating and coughing up lungs for a month. When I finally got back on my feet, I went to the cafeteria and it scared me to find the transition from frigid outdoor air into the heated indoor kind left my windpipe tight and me doubled-over hacking, struggling to inhale. I didn't know what was the matter, but that night after the cafeteria and every night that followed, whatever it was woke me up, gasping for breath, my face wet with the tears these fits induced.

One night, I stumbled from my bunk into the common bathroom to keep from tormenting my roommate. The deep, lacerating coughing wouldn't stop until I ran the shower scalding hot and stuck my face into the stall, sucking in the humid mist in greedy, desperate gulps. Slowly, my windpipe expanded and stopped whistling, and my heart stopped racing. It was around four in the morning when I left the showers.

"Yo, man, are you OK?" Matt, my hallmate, called from his room in his Brooklyn-Jewish stammer. He was up still, dressed in a METS SUCK T-shirt and loose Hoyas shorts, grooving to Coltrane—or maybe it was Miles or Bird, at the time I wouldn't have been able to tell—drinking bitter black coffee and scribbling his homework in between Napster downloads and trips to ESPN.com. The whole world was passed out except for him it seemed.

"I don't know what the fuck is going on with me," I said, glad to have someone to talk to.

"Come in, come in, and let me put some tea on for you, man; it'll open your lungs and help you sleep." Even though I had lived next door to Matt for months, I realized, we had never had a full conversation. I sipped the tea slowly and we politicked about a variety of topics I wouldn't have guessed I was interested in.

"You hear that backbeat right there, man?" he said, tapping his foot. "This shit is so sick."

"What's a backbeat?"

"You don't listen to jazz?"

"Nah, I guess I never have."

"Oh, man, I'll burn you some CDs."

"Word, please do," I said, aware all of a sudden that since I had

been old enough to purchase my own records it had never occurred to me to listen to anything other than hip-hop.

We sat that way for a while, admiring the drummer's skill, then
I thanked him for the Earl Grey, handed him his cup, and crawled
back into bed as the sun was coming up. For a period of time—
several days a week—this became our nightly ritual. Coughing, tea
and talking, and listening to music—black music like Miles Davis
and Nina Simone, which I was hearing for the first time. Eventually
I had a coughing fit so tough, no amount of steam would suppress
it. What I thought had been a passing fever had left me asthmatic.
But even after Flovent and albuterol replaced my hot shower and
tea routine, I continued dropping in on Matt and we became tight.

Matt and Rusty weren't flukes. Before long, I had a catholic
assortment of heads with whom I would chill: African, Jewish,
Hindu, WASP; East Coast, West Coast, Midwest, down-South; lower-
class, middle-class, upper-middle-class, richer-than-God. I don't
think I would have hung with most of them—in high school I
would have called them busters—were we not forced by the random nature of the Georgetown housing system into such close
proximity. But forced we were, and the friendships developed un-
expectedly and organically.

At the same time, it wasn't nearly as simple as that. I couldn't help
but notice that despite having been assigned to dormitories just as
diverse as mine, many of my black friends and classmates nonetheless remained socially cordoned off. This was a conscious decision
on their part, it occurred to me. During the week they ate and walked
to class among themselves. On weekends they danced and partied
together at house parties and at Howard. They were a self-selecting

minority on campus, segregating themselves to the back of the bus or over to the coloreds-only table when, if they chose, the fact was they could sit anywhere they pleased. Most of the black people I knew were polite and friendly to non-blacks, but there was something that fundamentally made them uncomfortable around them, too. What was that something? At the time, I didn't know. All I knew was that I no longer felt what they were feeling. And though I still spent most of my days kicking it with them, I found myself, to my surprise and for the first time in a long time, resisting the urge to join them fully in their seclusion.

Despite an abysmal first semester, I still attended class sporadically at best in the spring. Plenty of mornings degenerated into afternoons and then early evenings as I lamped in bed, BET thumping, the Big Tymers popping yellow bottles of Cristal and flashing iced-out grimaces, glaring at the camera lens, imploring all the young black men tuning in across the nation not to get to class but to get our roll on. I was basking—or drowning—in my sudden freedom, shirking the rigorous course load my years at Union Catholic had ill-equipped me to deal with, not heeding Pappy's call to stay on top of things from the jump.

The floors of Harbin Hall were deserted at these hours. All those party-it-up white boys in popped-collar Polos and Reef sandals— the ones who, naïvely, I had assumed were not handling their academic business either—were in fact in class. All of them except for Playboy. He skipped a hell of a lot, too, and he would come through my room and order food and play NBA 2K on my Dreamcast or use my TV to watch AC Milan play "football" and we would crack jokes and talk. I think that we were both glad to have the company.

Playboy was this tall, handsome, impossibly entitled kid with a sweeping brown cowlick and sad, jaded eyes, who at eighteen was dripping with the kind of I've-seen/-had/-bought/-tasted-everything ennui it takes several consecutive lifetimes to cultivate. He was not unassuming. He would have described himself as looking something like the Dickie Greenleaf character in *The Talented Mr. Ripley*. I had never met anyone like him: He seemed to be above money—was unconcerned with it as I've come to learn only people who are very used to having money can be unconcerned with having money, the way that only people who've never been sick can be unconcerned with having health. He spoke breezily of his apartments and homes in Paris, Venice, and Greece; of backyard sculpture gardens and Schieles on the wall; of the Tupac-namechecked boulevard back in California that bears his family's name; of household staff and family friends with names of their own, such as Steel, Picasso, Galliano, and Dunne. While most of us—white, black, and everything in between—were happy just to sit down in front of a hot cheesesteak, he dined out nightly and expensively at places like Cafe Milano, Peacock Cafe, and Bistro Français—and he complained about the food. The word around the hall was that on top of his allowance—a generous stipend by any standard—Playboy had figured out a way to siphon off extra funds, a little at a time, from each of his dad's credit cards and into a PayPal account he had set up for himself. That was the type of cat Playboy was. Of course, I had never even heard of PayPal; that was the type of cat I was.

For whatever reasons two people might click at any given moment in time, Playboy and I clicked. Maybe it was because, whether we were aware of it or not, neither of us quite fit into our assigned roles. He was an awkward Georgetown aristocrat, too well read and frankly too dissatisfied ever to blend with the happy-go-lucky sons and daughters of Greenwich bankers and cocky scions of Middle Eastern oil fortunes. And I was slowly, ever so slowly, awakening to the sense, which I couldn't articulate at the time, that there was more and I wanted more and I could have more than what Dr. Dre and Robert L. Johnson and Russell Simmons and my classmates at Union Catholic and in the small black corner of Georgetown and across town at Howard would have me believe.

In other words, Playboy needed grounding at the same time I needed elevation. We met each other somewhere in the middle. Still, it was difficult to venture off my own turf and to engage people like Playboy on their terms. The ice-grill mask of black cool and default membership within a hip-hop culture predicated on street sensibilities, elaborate shape-concealing costumes, and esoteric 'hood vernacular had shielded my boys and me from ever having to face up to the fact that we were not invincible or always in control of things. Rather than know ourselves, we cloaked our ignorance—like the rappers and thugs that we adored—in the rags of self-importance and faux-empowerment. It was so much easier to mime stereotypes than to invent ourselves as individuals. Making hip-hop culture the be-all end-all, dismissing everyone and everything not young and black out of hand was to reconfigure the world in our own familiar image—however unlikely it was that this image might jibe with reality. To relinquish this reconfiguration is to open oneself to a shitstorm of pain and insecurity; it is to allow someone else, possibly someone who has done more and seen more and received more than you have, to participate in the setting of criteria, in the determination of what is and is not good; it is to strip your feet of a life's worth of callus and step willingly onto the scorching pavement. And that is scary.

The sun hung low as a hot-air balloon over the Potomac as Playboy and I ambled down Prospect Street in search of food and a way to waste time. He suggested we make a right on Bank and roll to Dean & Deluca. I had seen the fancy white shopping bags with the black block lettering littered around campus, but I had never ventured inside.

"Trust me, it's good," Playboy said, and in we went. "What do you want to eat?"

"Whatever."

"OK, I'll go get the cheese. Can you grab a baguette?"

"Sure," I said, swiveling around only to realize as soon as he'd left that I didn't know what a baguette was. *Baguette . . . baguette . . . baguette . . .* I murmured to myself as if the steady repetition of the word might somehow conjure its hidden meaning. I had only heard the term used in reference to the diamonds encasing Puffy's Rolex or lodged in Mase's ear. I was at a loss now. I began to thread my way through aisle after pristine aisle of extra-virgin olive oils, colorful gelatos, and fine-ground espressos, confused and slightly embarrassed, in search of some hint or clue that might allow me yet to save face, but way too proud to ask any clerk for help. I had circled the whole store, making it all the way back to the front, when at last it hit me: *"Baguette" must just be French for "little bag."* It made perfect sense. He wants something to put all the shit in, I told myself. Why couldn't he just say that? When I returned with a small plastic hand basket, Playboy said, "Where's the baguette, dude?" I stared at him.

"This isn't it?" I said, pointing to the basket. He looked at me, and for a split second I saw his face shift: his jaw lowered just so as his lips parted and his eyes narrowed; his nose kind of scrunched and one eyebrow arched. The expression, which was gone as soon as it came, surprised and touched me like a slap, a slap whose resounding sting left marks across my face that spelled out my own ignorance. Or, more precisely, his face became a kind of bulletin board or mirror on which I was able to read that ignorance of mine—it was legible. He reached over and grabbed a powdery, oblong loaf of bread from a heaping pile and passed it to me.

The truth is, as with jazz, I had never before even thought about bread. Charles and I, Stacey, Moe over at Howard, the basketball thugs who threw gang signs around the cafeteria like chest passes, the girls who fawned over and serviced them—we talked about mad shit, discussed all types of things we deemed earth-shattering, like Iceberg sweatsuits and the appropriate time and place to flaunt jewelry, for example. But, it occurred to me in Dean & Deluca, we never talked about bread. Why not? Why didn't we ever think or talk about bread—or cheese, for that matter? No one *ever* talked about cheese. And why not? We ate three times a day, too, right? But that didn't matter. Real niggas didn't talk about cheese because, for whatever the reason, cheese ain't *real*. To be straight up, cheese is corny. Sneakers are real, not cheese; cognac is real, not wine; rap is real, not jazz; expensive cars are real, not expensive educations. My entire life I intuited and honored these little distinctions, as did all my friends. Bread, cheese, wine, books—though I talked about books with Charles and Pappy, that was the exception and because Pappy made us—I would never in a million years broach these subjects with Stacey or Ant; I simply understood not to. But now, one-on-one with Playboy in search of provisions and humiliated by my own ignorance, I wondered why that was: Who says cheese ain't real? Who gets to tell me that?

It's difficult to put into words the incredible smallness I felt as the result of such an otherwise inconsequential misunderstanding. I don't think it's frivolous to dwell on it, though, because our attitudes toward food often speak volumes. If you can't or don't bother to think broadly or curiously about what you ingest, then what else is passing you by? For my boys and me the answer was: a whole lot. It probably occurred to me at the time, too, that Playboy would not remember this fleeting little exchange, but that I would—and I *do*. Somewhere in this discrepancy of recollection—far more than in the discrepancy between our bank accounts or complexions—resides all the significance in the world.

As humbled as I felt, though, the fact is that just like in grade school, I retained real power over the situation, and I knew it. I had a choice right then, standing in the prepared foods section of Dean & Deluca, holding what I now knew was a baguette—I could take this experience in one of two directions. On the one hand, and with great ease, I could say "Yo, *fuck* a baguette—that shit is *gaaaay*, kid! Don't nobody eat no fucking baguette over here." And I could say it with a measure of bravado. I could play the whole thing off in a way that would make me look real and cool for not knowing about French breads and would put Playboy on the defensive for even having lived such an effete existence that he was so versed in such bitch-made-sounding baked goods. I could do that, I could strike that pose—and if I were with Charles or Ant and we could reinforce one another and make one big joke of the whole thing, that's probably exactly what I would do. That's the customary tack. On the other hand, I could try something new, new for me: I could swallow my pride and allow myself my curiosity and permit someone else to put me on to something unfamiliar.

That day, I realized I wanted more—to know more, taste more, see more, experience more. I was tired of trying to keep it real—real provincial—all the time. I dropped my guard, and the baguette, which we slathered with funky Brie and covered in fatty see-through-thin sheets of prosciutto di Parma, was delicious.

I was with Playboy several days later, chilling on the main lawn, squirting Super Soakers and trying to evade the muggy afternoon heat that always reminded me that D.C. used to be swampland, when I spotted Ashley approaching from the periphery. Ashley was this tall, buxom, high-yellow girl from the South, who belonged to a clique of pretty, upper-middle-class black female freshmen whose weakness for thugs, athletes, and rappers became the stuff of legend in the greater metropolitan area. The daughter of a dentist, probably a debutante, very Jack and Jill of America style—she was the kind of bourgeois black girl who never really had black friends or dated black guys growing up. The kind of black girl who had fallen in love in high school with the sort of white guy who dyes his hair red with little packets of cherry Kool-Aid and who doesn't normally even notice black chicks. In other words, she was the kind of hot, naïve, Hilary-from-*The-Fresh-Prince-of-Bel-Air* black girl every black guy, but especially every thugged-out black guy, at an elite white college is dying to fuck.

It didn't take long for her to realize her status at Georgetown atop the black social pecking order, to lose the white boy back home with the Kool-Aid in his hair, and to start converting all that sexual capital into tangible nights out and "dates." Maybe it took three months. What I know is that by the time she crossed my path on Copley Lawn that sweltering spring afternoon, she had been involved for some time with the Burkina Fasoian backup small forward on the basketball team to the chagrin of niggas everywhere. I didn't quite understand what all the fuss was about. Physically, Ashley was on point, and I would have counted myself among those aforementioned niggas who would gladly blaze. But personality-wise, she packed as much flavor as a bowl of white rice. At the time, I was nominally still with Stacey and, from where I stood, Ashley and her friends—dizzy broads with white accents and matching Bebe halter tops—literally and figuratively paled in comparison.

Maybe it was the hot sun glaring in my eyes. Maybe it was to impress Playboy or because I didn't think she could do anything about it that made me do it, I don't know. I only recall that as she strolled by and met my gaze I decided to unload nearly a full clip of Super Soaker fluid on her, turning her patterned summer dress into a thirsty sponge and reversing the powerful relaxing process in her hair like a stiff dose of black pride. She screamed: "You asshole!" I laughed so hard, the tears streamed as she stormed away, rattling off a string of pejoratives time or pride has not preserved for me.

"Dude, I can't believe you just did that," Playboy said, his eyes wide with surprise. "You totally just humiliated that girl!"

"Fuck her," I said, still laughing, and sat down on a bench nearby.

"Who is she even?" he asked, sitting down beside me and drap-
ing one long leg over the other.

"Man, she's nobody," I said.

That night as usual I went to New South with Dee to grab some
dinner. Dee was like my shadow back then. He was this sweet
kid with yellow, almost Chinese skin and long cornrows, which he
would tap instead of scratch when they itched so as not to disturb
the careful weave coursing across his scalp. He came from a very
rough part of D.C. ("the uhrea," he called it in his accent) and sometimes, when I heard him on the phone with his mother, I would
think it was his little sister or a neighborhood friend he was talking to. He lived below me in Harbin and buried himself in video
games, slam poetry, hardcore hip-hop, and sentimental R & B. He
had little to no money and mostly kept to himself. If I was at sea
with schoolwork, Dee was like a man overboard being ravaged
repeatedly against a wall of rock by the crashing surf. I liked Dee a
lot and I made it a point to include him in anything I was doing,
and I think he was grateful to me for that.

The two of us sauntered down the steps into the cafeteria, and
I noticed three or four basketball players milling around the foyer
in shower shoes and Hoyas sweats. I was friendly with two or
three players on the team, older heads, but the rest of them I said
what's up to and nothing more. These were what's-up guys. As
I rolled past, I threw the usual head nod their way and kept it moving. Then I felt a tug on my arm. The Burkina Fasoian had my wrist
locked in a vise grip; he wheeled me around. "Yo, the fuck is up?"
I said.

"You know what is up, my nigger," he said, sounding like a castrated Dikembe Mutombo in his melodic African-francophone English.

"Huh?"

"You cannot disrespect me like this, do you hear me?"

"I don't know what you're talking about."

"You cannot disrespect me!"

I wrenched myself loose from his astonishing grip. "What are you even talking about?"

"Today. This afternoon. You spray my girl. You cannot disrespect me like this." All of a sudden I realized why he was so hot. I had forgotten all about that. Now I looked around; his boys all were watching me. Dee looked nervous, but he was loyal and stood with me. Burkina Fasoian Dude was tall, like six-foot-six, but not scary. I had a difficult time believing he would get violent, and decided there was no way I could let him scold me.

"Man, fuck that bitch," I said with affected temerity and in a voice that sounded more like Charles's than mine. The Burkina Fasoian's eyes bulged, the vein on his neck popped like he was getting exercise, and before he could respond, one of his teammates, who up till that point had stayed off to the side, flew at me.

"Nigga, you better show some got'damn respect!" he said, with his Los Angeles inflection.

Now, this brother was enormous, played backup center—and if the Hoyas are known for anything at all, it is for their Herculean low-post. He was a legitimate seven feet, a jet-black Frankenstein—fearsome-looking, a brother you'd be seeing in your sleep. I didn't know this guy well, but some of the girls called him Free-to-Mess, because shortly after freshman orientation, he had told each of them individually that he was "free to mess." With his chest in my face, Free-to-Mess towered over me, glowering, munching on a bowl of Kellogg's Corn Pops, of all things.

"Whoa, whoa, whoa, this doesn't have nothing to do with you," I said to him, aware I may have gotten a little exuberant a moment earlier and catching out of the corner of my eye a glimpse of Dee, who, I noticed now, was even smaller than me!

"Nigga, you heard my patna; don't be disrespecting him like that again, dig?" Free-to-Mess said, shoveling Pops into his mouth, high up over my head, even as he spoke. I didn't say anything, wasn't trying to escalate the situation. "He won't fight you, feel me? But I'm red-shirted this year, nigga, I will."

The third player, who remained seated on the stairs, blue bandana tied neatly around his clean-shaven head, didn't say a word, looked at me. I scanned my brain for plausible options. What would Charles do? Charles might actually throw down, try to snuff the giant in the solar plexus and then play it as it came. Well, that was a universe of pain I wasn't trying to visit. What would Pappy do? Pappy never would be in this situation in the first place, fool! My heart plummeted through me like a cinder block.

"Nigga, say I won't just pour these Co'n Pops all on top of yo' head, patna? Then whatchu gonna do?" Free-to-Mess was egging me on now, and I knew enough about these things to know that it was time to leave.

"Man, whatever," is all I could manage to mumble, and I broke toward the public space of the dining room, firing off one of those God-if-only-you-let-me-get-out-of-this-I'll-be-good-I-promise appeals, praying Free-to-Mess would let it drop and not follow me inside talking shit in front of everyone in the cafeteria. Meanwhile Dee, who had spent weeks with all these players in the extra-help summer session for black and Latino students on the edge, said something conciliatory on my behalf, and to my relief they walked off in the opposite direction.

I ate a quick, tasteless dinner, then excused myself from Dee's company and shut myself inside my room. My nerves were on fire, temples throbbing with anger and a lot of wounded pride. I had come to Georgetown thinking things like this couldn't happen anymore. That I would be tough and everyone else would be soft. Yet there I was, back in the same position I had been in a year earlier with Jerry, only now I was on my own. I snatched the cordless phone off my roommate's desk and dialed a fraction of Charles's number up in New England before slamming the receiver back down on its base. Charles was in school, too, and he had his own shit to deal with. He wasn't my keeper. I sat back down; I didn't know what to do.

What was I *supposed* to do? Was I supposed to call my boys back home who didn't go to college? Call Stacey and have her get one of her drug-dealing cousins to come down? Call my brother and see if any of his or Michael's peoples from the military—older dudes who smoked and drank hard and considered me a little brother—might come up? This was foolish as hell and I knew it; I was in college, not in the street. Why was I fronting like I was in the street? Why did I always front like I was in the street?

Of course Pappy was no longer at my side to guide me, and I missed him something awful right then. I wanted to sit across the chessboard from him and search his face for answers. As I sat in my room fuming, I thought about him and I could hear his voice inside my head: "Son, slow down and think. Remember Bismarck's balanced-alternatives approach? Always keep more than one arrow in your quiver." Such lines never could hold a candle to Tupac's When-We-Ride-on-Our-Enemies philosophy in the mind of a black teen with raging hormones and sometimes-violent girl problems. Yet here I was, years later, recalling Pappy's words, not Pac's. They must have seeped in deeper than I had known. "You don't immediately have to respond to anyone, and sometimes your response can be not to respond at all," I could hear him say. "You have an option A, an option B, an option C, an A-1, A-2, A-3, son; take your time, be cool. Don't react blindly; don't allow anyone to make you jump; keep your options open." Pappy's Bismarckian flow spouted and welled in my head as though a stopper had been loosed. What if my option A was not to respond at all? I asked myself.

As the days went by and the calendar continued to flip, nothing further came of my confrontation with the bottom of the Hoya bench. None of the players stepped to me again or bothered me in any way. And yet I wasn't in the clear by any means. When I sat down at the black tables in the cafeteria, no one really looked me in the eye. I felt like my jokes drew less laughter than they used to. I received fewer and fewer invitations to chill. I swore I could detect eyes rolling in my direction and shit-talk rippling out from behind my back, lapping against my ears. More and more, it began to sink in: I had been excommunicated from the black community at Georgetown. Of course, I still had my boys: Pup, Dee, some upperclassmen and -women who were so close to graduating they no longer kept up with campus gossip. These were my black friends. But by and large, there were no two ways about it. I was an outcast, an untouchable, no longer at home or welcome in the only micro-cosm I had ever bothered to know.

When I had attacked Ashley with my water gun, I couldn't really say why I hated her so much; the feeling was far more vis-ceral than it was rational. I acted on a whim, an unthinking desire. Had I been in the presence of another black friend, I am sure I would have suppressed it completely. But standing there with Play-boy, an outsider, a guy who didn't and truly couldn't understand all the vagaries of the caste system I lived in, I felt all of a sudden moved to rebel against this hierarchy, not just to reject it but also to defile it. I think I felt compelled to reject and defile whatever part of myself there was that still believed in it.

Thrust into my new role as persona non grata in Georgetown black society, the more I marinated on the significance of this ran-dom, pathetically melodramatic turn of events in my life, the more the absurdity of the situation started to press its full weight upon me. For as far back as I could think, I had followed and tried to fit in with cats who seemed black, who seemed real, to the exclusion of all else. I had allowed these brothers on TV and on my block—the majority of whom did not have shit figured out—to participate in my own self-definition. As a child I worshiped what I saw on BET. In high school, I still worshiped what I saw on BET and I rolled with a posse of self-proclaimed "niggers" who were not going to make it and they knew it. Now, at an elite private college, I *still* worshiped what I saw on BET, and I had spent the majority of my first year barely getting by academically, killing myself to belong in a hierarchy whose ruling caste was made up of C-walking swing guards and forwards and their coed sycophants, some of whom could freestyle at house parties but could not read at grade level.

Was any of this what Pappy had sent me to college to achieve: To watch and emulate BET all day? To clash with a seven-foot Southern Californian wielding a bowl of Corn Pops? To debate an enraged and rumored-to-be-impotent African, who, all things considered, was really a pretty nice guy but who was trying as hard as I was to fit in and be hard? Had I really come all the way to Georgetown just to hop over to Howard any chance I could get in hopes of peeping a large butt or Cam'ron or some lesser-known MC? No, no, no, of course not—this wasn't it.

CHAPTER SIX

You Can't Go Home Again

You can't go home again. From where I sat in the driver's seat, Stacey to the right of me, there was a whole lot of truth in those five words. "Why did you buy those shoes?" she wanted to know. She was referring to the black leather Pradas I'd just exchanged a week's salary for. "And them pants, those shits is so . . . tight." I had begun dressing differently; buying new clothes with the money I was making doing temp work at KPMG in Short Hills, New Jersey. According to one of my brother's friends I was beginning to resemble "a gay poet."

"Do you know I'm actually a twenty-eight waist?" I asked Stacey. "All these years I've been wearing a thirty-six, I didn't even know my right size." I looked over at her. The most familiar face in the world. Somehow it was one of the strangest now, too. She was eighteen, all curves and ripe flesh with copper in it, fresh out of high school, no plans, hadn't bothered to take the SAT, didn't care. "I think we should take a trip to Italy or France or somewhere, see some shit, you know?" I said, really just to have something to say.

"Italy, nigga? Them white niggas at school got you buggin'," she said.

I laughed. "Why not?"

She rolled her eyes.

Since the day I met her when I was fifteen, I wanted her anytime I saw her. Now was no different. My right hand rested on her left thigh. I pulled the car into an empty corner of Tamaques Park, took out the keys, and kissed her. She tasted like bubble gum. I probably tasted like San Pellegrino, which I'd started drinking all the time and which was harder to find in our part of Jersey than in Georgetown. We fucked in the backseat of the car, but she was gone, off in another world I couldn't come to.

"What's wrong?" I said when I finished.

"Nothing," she said, looking into the distance, refastening the buttons on her fly. She could fill out a pair of Miss Sixtys like no one I had ever known. I flicked the condom out the window, put the car in reverse, turned the music all the way up.

It was just getting dark when we got to Pup's crib in Maplewood. I had a lot of trouble finding it, missed several turns, went back and forth on what turned out to be the correct road at least four times before breaking down and asking for directions at a Mobil station. "Don't you know where you goin'?" Stacey said in a tone I found less than friendly.

"No, it's been a minute since I've been out around this way," I confessed. She sucked her teeth and drummed her acrylic nails against the wood grain in the armrest. It was a habit of hers, which up until then I hadn't noticed drove me crazy. The attendant explained to me my error, and we were off.

Pup came downstairs, gave me a pound, and climbed into the backseat. He had grown up in Newark, not far from where we were, then got shipped in ninth grade to a little Christian boarding school somewhere in rural Pennsylvania, far from the Jupiterian pull of the corner, which his parents knew was powerful enough to drag brothers right out of their houses and into its orbit like tiny satellites. Pup told me once that his father drove taxis in Manhattan. I don't know what his mother did. Somehow the two had managed to put all three of their sons through boarding school and college (his brothers were at Duke), which seemed to me like a kind of miracle.

At Georgetown, Pup and I lived across the bathroom from each other, the only black kids on our floor. We became fast friends over video games, pickup basketball, and midnight hero sandwiches. He was a different kind of black than I had ever known—first-generation, the son of Ghanaian immigrants, not the descendant of Southern slaves like Stacey and me. He had another culture, another point of reference; the images he saw here weren't addressing him specifically. Which is to say, he hadn't been taught to despise himself from the moment he could talk the way Stacey had been and the way I would have been were Pappy not so hell-bent on preventing that from happening. Which is also to say, he was African-American (in the literal sense) as much as he was black. The difference such an accident of time and birth can make, I was learning, is both subtle and difficult to overestimate.

Besides that, Pup was short and muscle-bound, bald, the color of a Hershey bar, and the owner of an infectious laugh. I'd seen him disarm the hardest brothers and the aloofest white boys with the same easy smile. His presence in the car, as the poet said, momentarily evaporated whatever disagreeables hung in the air between Stacey and me. The three of us sped up the Parkway toward Mary's house in Glen Ridge.

All day I had ricocheted between fits of excitement and stark raving terror at the thought of bringing Stacey with me to a party full of college friends—all of whom, with the exception of Pup and some Indian kid named Raj, were white. "Do you want to meet some of my friends?" I'd asked her the day before, trying to sound mad casual, expecting she'd say no.

"I don't care either way," she told me. "If you want me to come, I'll come."

Shit went sour from the drop. "Would you like a beer or something to drink?" I heard a girl ask Stacey as we walked through the kitchen and out onto the back deck.

"No," was all she replied, with no smile and disinclined to let the conversation proceed any further than it had, which was nowhere. There was even something belligerent about the way she said it. The girl flashed a sheepish grin and looked dejected or confused. Pup stepped in and made her laugh and I heard their laughter behind me as I shut the screen door.

"Why can't you just chill and be nice, baby?" I whispered in Stacey's ear as we went to a wooden bench and sat on it, overlooking the rolling green of the deep, landscaped lawn. I thought the lawn looked nice.

"The bitch asked me if I wanted a drink, I said no, what the fuck else do you want?" Stacey snapped. The look on her face—how many times have I seen that look; and on how many faces like Stacey's? It was this wall of a look that said, among other things: I'm not interested in you at all.

It didn't take long for me to realize that night that my two worlds—what was left of my Union Catholic past and what looked like my Georgetown future—were about as easy to fit together as square pegs and triangular holes. The more I tried to coax Stacey into sociable conversation, the more she fortified her wall. I felt a mixture of embarrassment and resentment toward her. It wasn't that she did or said any one specific thing I could pinpoint, or anything that taken on its own would constitute such an egregious affront. It was more like there was this air about her, a certain *steez* or way of carrying herself, an antisocial steez, which made her cold and hard, uncivil.

Like almost all of my old friends, Stacey was a paradox. She had grown up middle-class in a leafy section of Plainfield with two cars parked behind the motorized garage door and a refrigerator full of steak and Asti Spumante (a sparkling white wine of questionable taste, sure, but a sparkling white wine all the same!). An illiterate Chinese rice farmer in a paddy field or a São Paulo orphan in a favela scrap heap would be hard-pressed to differentiate Stacey's lot from Mary's. But economics doesn't explain everything. It would be equally true to say that in Camden, Newark, or Harlem, Stacey was no interloper. She could blend into the most poverty-stricken black ghettos like a spotted leopard in the sub-Saharan brush—seamlessly—and not just owing to the color of her skin, but also because she possessed the requisite savoir faire to navigate that forbidding terrain. She had a very convincing street pose, a pose that she, like all of us at one point or another, had to learn and to master (no one's born that way)—a pose that now she either wouldn't or couldn't turn off. Perhaps she'd been doing it so long it wasn't even a pose anymore; that was also a possibility.

The way she was acting was as familiar to me as my face—how many times had I myself tried to be like this?—and at the same time it was new, new from this vantage, newly incomprehensible. The pose no longer seemed so irresistible to me; it was ridiculous or gratuitous all of a sudden, anything but cool. Observing her on the deck that night, far away from her usual habitat, I felt my nose close; her hold on me was broken. For the very first time since we had met, I could imagine myself without her. Whatever stamp of approval her presence on my arm had provided me in the past, I no longer felt I needed it. The rest of the party, as far as it involved Stacey and me, is a haze of forced smiles and awkward speechlessness.

After I dropped off Pup, I drove Stacey to her mother's in Plainfield in what started as silence and escalated into shouts and screams. She hated what I was becoming—had already become. It was "wack" and I wasn't "the same" anymore. There was "another nigga" in the picture now, too, she revealed. I had begun to expect that. Tell me something I don't know, I thought. He was a thug, "real thorough," she bragged. They had met at a cookout or a birthday party for her girlfriend in Roselle or someplace like that. He asked her number and she said what the hell. I was down in D.C. at the time, doing whatever it was that I did in college with fools like Playboy, she reasoned, and she was lonely or curious or bored—

and what did I expect, really? Did I not see this coming while I was running around using "big-ass words" like life was some giant spelling bee, talking "that bullshit" and dressing "like a fag fresh out the Village"? It was my fault, not hers, she said. I didn't say anything, just ground my teeth (nervous habit) and tried to keep the car steady on the road, which was no small task.

Then she told me something that I didn't know: "I'm pregnant, nigga. I missed my period last month and an EPT test confirmed that shit." My heart practically leaped onto the dashboard; Pappy's worst fear made flesh, I thought, only thank Jesus or Jah or Allah I had been in another part of the country when it happened. It's not yours, I told myself, but the revelation still caught me obliquely like a sucker punch to the side of the head. I was dazed.

"You're what!" I screamed, hurling the car to a stop on the road's shoulder and smacking the button for the hazards like it had stolen something from me. I cut the ignition and took a deep breath, trying with what might I could channel through my gaze to grip Stacey with my eyes and wring out any last droplet of familiarity from her defiant and unrecognizable face. There was none left. She was pregnant, she repeated matter-of-factly, as though she were telling me she had hay fever or oily skin, and there was contempt in her eyes, not remorse. She loved her baby's father and had decided to keep the child and move to Newark, and that was that.

"You're having the baby and moving to Newark. Are you serious?" I said, sounding more like a concerned parent than the lover I had been just hours ago. As my mind raced, my stomach felt like a tangle of drawstrings being pulled tighter from every direction. "You don't work! How are you going to support a child? You're only eighteen! What does this motherfucker even do?"

"Nigga, he sells crack!" she shrieked, and her voice and that wall she had so meticulously erected fractured. "He be on the block. What the fuck do you do, huh? You think you better than niggas 'cause you fucking go to college? Fuck you!"

I couldn't tell whether she was telling me the truth or simply trying to amplify my pain, but I let the interrogation drop right there. How do I argue with that? What logical assertions do I posit against that? And what would be the point? "Well, I hope you'll be very happy," is all I could say, and the car plunged into a deep silence like the lull that precedes a tsunami, like the slow, peaceful quiet that comes over the ocean as it draws itself back and readies to devour. Soon, but not quite yet, the destruction would be total, and whatever we had shared would be wiped away; I knew that. For the moment, though, we sat there, Stacey and me, side by side, locked in a miserable stalemate or undeclared truce. The orangey light from a streetlamp filtered through the moon roof and glared off the wetness on her cheeks. It must have shone from mine, too.

I deposited Stacey in her mother's driveway, and when she got out she slammed the door violently. The sound echoed with the ring of finality. I turned off my cell phone to prevent myself from calling after her, after the girl I had loved very imperfectly for four years, and pulled out of there—out of her driveway and out of that part of my life. I let the cool night air whip through the window and wash over my face as I drove. The air felt good, and I decided not to go straight home. I drove around for what seemed like hours, through Plainfield, through the black sides of Fanwood and Scotch

Plains and Westfield, through the side streets we had driven together so many times before on the way to the mall or to the movies, past the familiar houses of all the boys and girls who only a year ago had defined my horizons for me and who now I knew I wouldn't see again. I drove and I thought about Stacey.

I remembered when her brother was born and they took him home from the hospital and she held the little boy in her arms and looked happy and proud and nothing like a mother, but rather like a child herself—just a good-looking child—as she stroked the baby's trembling little back and kissed his fat, flushed cheeks. I remembered when, after she had won some local beauty pageant in Rahway or Linden or someplace like that, her family and I piled into her mother's red Tahoe and headed to the nearest Applebee's to celebrate and Stacey put her arm around me in the backseat and said shyly, "See, I got some talent," and this girl, this fucked-up girl who lived like tomorrow didn't matter, seemed like the sweetest thing in the world to me right then.

I remembered, too, when Pappy tried in vain for nearly a month to get Stacey to be serious about school, convincing her skeptical mother to let him tutor her daughter in the evenings for free, after he had finished a full day with his paying clients. Why on earth did he assign himself *that* thankless task? It was in part an unspoken favor to me, but in part I also think it was simply because black girls like Stacey just break Pappy's heart. I imagine on some level they must remind him of his own beautiful teenage mother. He had been too young to heal or protect her when she could have used a Pappy badly.

Every night after Stacey left our house, with Pappy's pink and pastel green test-prep material nestled under her arm—which everyone including Stacey knew she would never use, and which Pappy photocopied and gave her anyway—Pappy would tap on my bedroom door. He'd ask if he could come in, and would shake his head, saying things like *You know, Stacey's eyes just light the whole room* and *She has such a smile when she wants to have one; she really is very smart, you know* and *She's got a sharp memory, but I'm afraid that girl will never do the kind of work it takes to put that mind to any good use; she doesn't want to do it, it's that simple.* And I remembered knowing how right he was and feeling sad and like I wanted to protect Stacey myself, but understanding full well, as my father must have understood about his mother, that what was coming for her was more powerful than anything I could summon against it.

This is how I would like to remember my girl Stacey, then—sweet, smart, and innocent like a child, with big bright eyes that lit the room and a smile that made Pappy smile—but I cannot. In a different context, maybe, but in the context we grew up in, all the noises inside her head and outside her door snuffed out her potential before she even had breasts or hair underneath her arms. By eighteen, she was a statistic: another undereducated, unwed black teen mother doing her small part to bolster the 70 percent single-mother birthrate everyone bemoans.

I doubt I would have realized all this that night in the car, but it's true all the same: In the sixty-three years between the moment when my smart and talented grandmother had Pappy at seventeen, embarrassing her family and her church by doing so, and the moment when Stacey got pregnant at the turn of the millennium, becoming too cool for school and embarrassing no one, black life had changed in dramatic ways. Human and civil rights were in, hip-hop was in, nihilism was in, self-pity was in, the street was in, and pride and shame were out—two more cultural anachronisms confined to the African-American dustbins of history, like jazz music and zoot suits. Whether I knew all that then or not, I knew enough to sense that this was not the way things should be. When I got home in the middle of the night, I woke up my parents and let them know that I was safe.

That was the start of a strange and lonely summer for me. I often had difficulty sleeping that summer. At night I dreamed that I was losing my teeth. I would wake up startled, cupping my mouth and panting. During the day, I either went to work at my dismal data entry job or hid out at my parents' house. Clarence was living at home then, too, but he worked the graveyard shift doing tech support out in White Plains and our paths seldom seemed to cross.

Occasionally, I did see Charles, though not that often. Under Pappy's guidance he and I had applied mostly to the same schools and pledged to each other that we would go wherever we both were admitted, regardless. When it became clear that I had gotten into better schools than Charles, I didn't even hesitate to break the agreement (sometimes I think he would have done the same thing, other times I'm not so sure). We entered our respective schools both with an eye toward econ majors, the same vision of lavish Wall Street paychecks dancing in our heads like sweet sugarplums or thick video hoes. The similarities stopped there, however. He had done extraordinarily well that first year, much better than I had done, and the experience of going away hadn't jarred him as it had me. When school let out, he slid back into his neighborhood and his old routines without friction—smoothly—almost like he'd never left. He knew how to turn it on and off, I guessed. Why couldn't I?

The first few times we hung out were awful, stilted affairs. We were like two people who have run out of things to say to each other but who make a go at it anyway, either because it seems the right thing to do or because not to do so would extinguish the relationship outright, and that is frightening. We used to finish each other's sentences in high school, but now it was as though he spoke Latin and I spoke Cantonese. The times he visited my house, it occurred to me he was really coming to see my father. This irritated me as much as it did when on the flimsiest pretext he used my computer to check his final grades (dean's list). I was in no hurry to look up my own marks in front of him (academic probation). Charles and I were on two separate pages of perhaps two different books; I began to worry, which was true but not entirely. The truth is that when shit hit the fan with Stacey, it was Charles I called and it was Charles who took it upon himself to lift my spirits.

"First of all, she's just a bitch," he reminded me over the phone the day after my disastrous trip to Glen Ridge. He was eating some crunchy piece of fruit and talking with his mouth full, very calmly, very authoritatively. "Bitches are like yellow lights, son: You just run through them."

"Yeah, I know, I know," I said, "but the thing is—"

"You *have* to keep that in mind at all times, nigga, I'm serious!" he erupted, taking another bite and pausing to regain the composure he momentarily had lost. "OK, Thomas? You gotta do that, bro."

"OK."

"All right. Second of all, and this is for your own good, I'm tak-ing you to a strip club tonight to prove to you once and for all that bitches are all the same. Trust me, I know this."

He scooped me that evening in his mother's navy blue Nautica minivan and we drove out to some far-flung shit hole in Sayreville or Perth Amboy, where it reeked of cigarettes and beer, as if a chain-smoking janitor had mopped the floors with buckets of Bud-weiser. Most of the dancers were Puerto Rican or ethnic white and most of the clientele were upward of forty and obese.

"See? All the same," he said, motioning around him as we took seats at the horseshoed stage. On it, a gorgeous Latina with an I'm-not-even-in-this-room expression sank to her knees and trans-formed herself—like an X-rated Decepticon—from a woman into a receptacle for crumpled dollar bills and jeers. A bleach-blond waitress wearing a low-cut tank top asked us what we'd have to drink. I'm not sure what I ordered, but it must have been soft since I had never gotten around to getting a fake ID. We sat there for a while, swapping theories on how pretty women end up in such disgusting spots, nursing our Cokes or Sprites, laughing like old times. Then Charles said, "Pick a girl, any one; I'll buy you a dance." I excused myself to go to the bathroom and when I came back I said I wanted the snow white Boricua in the corner with the pil-lowy breasts and tongue ring. Charles called her over, whispered something in her ear, and she led me by the hand to a back room that was half-obscured from the main floor by a dusty black velvet curtain, which didn't completely close.

Through the gap between the curtain and the wall I could make out Charles, silhouetted against the black light radiating from the stage. He was staring at me with a strange look on his face, I thought, though it was too dark to say for sure just what that look might mean. He must have told the girl I had gotten dumped, because the first thing she said to me was that she would make me forget whoever had broken my heart. "Thank you," I said, and she straddled my legs and took off her top. She smiled at me sympathetically and it was impossible to tell how old she was.

As she gyrated, I neither forgot Stacey nor became convinced all bitches were the same. For example, this one's chest, which she told me if I touched would cheer me up, was far larger and more beautiful than Stacey's, but Stacey made me laugh in a way I used to think was priceless. That was a significant difference, I thought, and the truth is that I missed Stacey badly right then. I missed the real Stacey, not the hardened street chick I had brought with me to Mary's party. The real Stacey, the shy girl with the talent, she was inhumed somewhere deep beneath layers and layers of hollow facades, like one of those Russian nesting dolls.

I tried to keep my thoughts off Stacey, though, and told the Puerto Rican on my lap that she was probably right. I cupped her in my hands and let her earn her money. She felt extremely soft, softer than a regular girl, with that invisible stripper film of baby powder, lotion, and sweat coating her freshly shaved skin and grinding into the fabric of my jeans. When the dance had ended, she stroked my face and asked if I was better now. "Yes," I lied, and I decided to pay her myself instead of asking Charles for the money.

"Want to see something?" she said. I nodded and she pulled her bikini to the side and pointed to where her clitoris was pierced.

The way she did it, with great care and even a little pride, was unspeakably sad, and I couldn't tell whether she was just passing time between dances or revealing her deepest secret to me.

Did I learn anything tonight? I wondered after we had left. Yes, several things. I learned that women are more powerful than hangovers, and there is no sexual hair of the dog to numb the ache. I learned that no one—not bitches or niggas—is really the same. I learned that I was not Charles nor could I ever be, and though I loved him like a brother (I knew that, too), it would be in my interest to stop mimicking him—and sooner rather than later. I was fine with all of those things, it occurred to me.

"Oh, you know what, my dude?" Charles said to me once we had gotten back on Route 9, "Abyss is right over there. You remember that fucking place?" *In My Lifetime Vol. 1* knocked on the car stereo. Charles had been rapping along to it as he drove, not doing whole verses, which he knew by heart, but improvisationally finishing lines here and there, like a hype man at a concert or an ad-libber in the booth. "How real is this?" Jay-Z asked rhetorically through the speakers and Charles echoed from the driver's seat. Jay's pitch was high and Charles's was low, but they both spoke with the same tone of assurance, a remarkable self-assurance, it seemed to me.

I could see the parking lot surrounding Club Abyss looming on the horizon and swarming with bumper-to-bumper traffic. We had to slow as we passed. Most of the cars and trucks pulling in were souped-up whips, with big chrome rims and low-profile tires. Some had miniature TV screens set into the backs of their headrests, which flashed changing colors or cast a consistent glow through the tinted rear windows. The ones that gave off a steady light had nothing playing on them; they were simply turned on. They had no function but to broadcast their own existence into the empty, indifferent night. Back in the day, I recalled, Club Abyss had seemed a kind of cathedral—a high church of ass and mystery and adventure—or some vague opportunity, a chance to test out how cool and down I was, to put to use the body language and slang I had been rehearsing in front of the mirror and at school. But from the road this night, it didn't look like any of that. It just looked like a desperate box in the middle of nothing, a forgettable blemish on the side of an ugly thoroughfare that connected one nowhere to the next.

"Should we go and check it out?" Charles asked.

"Nah, I'm too tired," I said, looking out the window of his mother's minivan at the neon lights creeping by.

"Well, do you at least feel better now?" he asked, and I could feel his eyes on me.

"Yeah, I do," I said, and that was the truth.

As the summer wore down, I spent most of my free time taking walks with my mother—long, meandering, soul-searching walks through Fanwood and Scotch Plains, around the high school, around the elementary school where Clarence had been menaced, through the park—long, peaceful walks that weaved through streets so familiar I could close my eyes and get home were it not for the traffic. Or I played chess with my father, sometimes for hours on end, before taking my leave and digging through his vast library, reading, reading book after book after book until I fell asleep by myself in my room. I had lived in the midst of written treasure for nineteen years somehow without ever having noticed it, I realized that summer, as if the books in our house used to be wrapped in invisible dust jackets or hidden behind mirrors.

But that's an exaggeration—of course I had seen them; they were everywhere. Startled friends would point them out to me when they came over, timidly, as if they thought Pappy was a sadist and this was his torture chamber. There were also those times when my brother and I joked that Pappy's shelves were like a kind of fucked-up wallpaper (they completely blocked all the walls) or a cruel obstacle course through which we were forced to maneuver like clumsy gerbils (they partially blocked some of the doors). Why couldn't we just have a normal living room with a home theater in it like so-and-so or so-and-so, we sometimes asked the gods to no discernible answer. Most of the time, though, we didn't complain about the piles of books or pay them any mind. They were simply there, a physical reality that was not good or bad, just a fact, like a chandelier or a potted plant.

As a child I lived with the sense that my aloofness toward his books didn't just bother Pappy—it hurt him deeply. I couldn't understand why, though. "Why does Pappy get so intense about the freaking reading?" I asked my mother when I was eleven or twelve. "I already do all the work he gives me, I'm not getting into trouble, my friends' fathers would be beyond happy!" I said with a sense of self-pity. At this, my mother, a gentle and easygoing woman, removed her glasses and fixed me with an intense look that took me by surprise:

"Honey, those books ... Are. Your. Father's. Life. You have no idea how hard he had to work, what he had to go through, just to get his hands on them. What kind of hell he caught—his own family told him an educated nigger in the South was a dead nigger. Do you realize he hid himself in the closet with a flashlight in order to read? Baby, you cannot imagine the world he has lived in, and you should thank God that you can't."

All my life I heard things like this, disconnected bits and pieces, fragments of justification, sometimes vividly painful vignettes, sometimes hauntingly vague allusions to Pappy's younger days and what he had endured in the South and beyond. As a child who was encouraged and even bribed to flourish and realize myself, I took Pappy's pain almost for granted: Things were harder in the olden days, right? I couldn't wrap my mind around the injustice; it was alien to me. Surely things couldn't be that bad, I thought, pushing the imagery out of my mind, out of my way. But that summer at my parents' house, a guest now and no longer a tenant, I began to revisit those stories I had heard as a child and to see them anew, with fresh eyes, with a new curiosity, and with a new sense of horror.

One goes as follows: In 1959 Pappy was twenty-two, completely alone, just out of college, and doing graduate work in sociology at Cal State, Los Angeles. He was also looking for a job to pay the bills. One day he showed up at a government building downtown to take an aptitude test for some civil-service position he had seen advertised in the newspaper. The commute was easy, the work was interesting, and the pay was good. Inside the building, in a large room where the test was being given, there were numerous applicants, thirty or more, and one administrator, a young Chinese or Korean woman who was seated alone up front. The way it worked, applicants walked from the back, where they entered, up to the front, where the administrator waited, and were given copies of the test and some instructions and told to take a seat. When Pappy's turn came and he reached out for his test, the Asian woman picked up a copy from the pile, same as she had for everyone else, but instead of handing it over to Pappy, she held it out in front of her and then tore the paper in half, slowly, purposefully, in a noisy and exaggerated motion that made the other test takers look up from their work.

"What's going on?" Pappy asked, though I suspect he knew full well what was happening.

"We don't have any tests for niggers," she announced matter-of-factly, staring him in the face.

It was a jolting, graphic kind of bigotry, which, when I picture it, seems almost cinematic in that sunny Tinseltown setting, like something possible only in a movie—only in a fucked-up *noir*. Accustomed to blunt racism but unable to grasp what he had personally ever done to invite such naked hatred, Pappy was devastated but resolved not to allow his antagonist the victory of seeing him broken and diminished.

"I see, well, thank you for your time, then," was all he said, and he picked up his briefcase with a forced poise no twenty-two-year-old I know will ever need to muster. The walk from the front of the room to the back and out the door, he says, was one of the longest and most self-conscious of his life. A half-century later he can scarcely discuss the episode without vibrating in rage.

Not long after that, Pappy found a job at an insurance company for which he was grossly overqualified. The commute was long, about twice the distance that it would have been to the government gig, and it involved a combination of walking and riding the bus. The pay was also less. But the insurance company was willing to hire blacks, and Pappy took the position without having to think about it very hard.

In the evenings, after work and late into the night, he studied for school and also for himself. He studied until his eyes went out and sometimes he fell asleep with his shoes on. There were stretches—weeks, sometimes even months—when money was so scant, he ate peanut butter by the spoonful for breakfast and lunch. Good source of protein, he said. And also, by forgoing meals, he could still buy books: *The Wretched of the Earth*, by Frantz Fanon; *The Crisis of the Negro Intellectual*, by Harold Cruse; *The Collected Short Stories of Eudora Welty*; *The Theory of the Leisure Class*, by Thorstein Veblen; *Candide*, by Voltaire; *The Division of Labor in Society*, by Emile Durkheim; *The House of Mirth*, by Edith Wharton; *The Sun Also Rises*, by Ernest Hemingway; *Great Short Works of Edgar Allan Poe*; *The Metamorphosis and Other Stories*, by Franz Kafka; *The Complete Works of Guy de Maupassant*. Pappy never believed in God; reading was his lone salvation. Nor did he simply amass books or peruse them; he *strove* with them in the full religious sense of the word that Kierkegaard intended—he fought these texts as if his life were at stake—which, in a way, it was.

When I was growing up, if you were to walk into my father's library and pick up one of his books at random, you would see on the inside cover, written in a careful hand, Pappy's signature hovering above the precise date and location of purchase ("Clarence

Leon Williams, January 6, 1973, Days in Spokane" or "CLW, November 18, 1965, Santa Monica"). Which is to say, you would catch a glimpse of the reverence with which this Southerner from the wrong side of the color line regarded the object in your hand. If you were to thumb through the book, you would notice other things, too: margins overrun with ink, questions demanded, allusions uncovered, arcana circled and defined, arguments digested and broken down, rebuttals and counterarguments sustained and advanced—you would see a probing mind, the mind of what society had designated a nigger, waging intellectual warfare. You would see acts of civil disobedience (whether they were violent or not would only depend on your perspective).

If you were to walk several paces beyond Pappy's study, back into my bedroom, however, and sift through the stacks of *Vibe* magazines, the towers of CDs and mountains of Nike Airs, and come upon some of *my* books, you would see something else entirely. You would see pristine texts that had not been hard-won but that had been given to me (Plutarch's *Lives*, say). Inside the cover there would be the same familiar handwriting ("To—Thomas Chatterton Williams; From, Pappy, with best wishes—always! Dec. 6, 1995, Days at Fanwood, New Jersey *Note: These are lives worth studying carefully.") If you were to flip through the pages, though, you would see only evidence of absence, a lack of marginalia and wear and tear, a kind of apophatic argument, a mind unaware of what so recently was at stake, a perfunctory mind, the mind of a comfortable and pampered teenager who just happened to be black—the way he happened to be skinny and happened to have long fingers—and against whom society hardly could be said to hold an insurmountable grudge; you would see a mind that had been going through the motions. You would see a mind that didn't think books were very *cool*.

It was only after living in Georgetown and coming back to Fanwood that I could understand what it was all about. I could finally step back and see Pappy's library for all the books in it and begin to recognize what exactly he had been trying to share with me. I had to go away to appreciate this. It had been too overwhelming for me as a child. Pappy's books held our house under a perpetual siege; the house itself was his library. The study was the heart, with shelves and tables buckling (literally) beneath the weight of his books: to the left from the front door, leaning floor-to-ceiling shelves of Negro literature, African-American polemics, slave narratives, and black sociology; to the right, a wide, low shelf like an open credenza of Chinese and Japanese history, Russian literature, and some Southern literature (Faulkner, O'Connor, Harper Lee, Capote—if you consider him Southern); in recessed shelving above that, rows of short stories and plays (Mary McCarthy, Salinger, Tennessee Williams, Sophocles); against the far wall, behind the desk, two large tables holding on for dear life under the weight of centuries of classical and western European philosophical thought; on the desk, a constantly updated selection of flavors-of-the month (*The House of Rothschild*, a Hannah Arendt reader, *The 48 Laws of Power*) and perennial favorites (*The Story of Philosophy*, various Foucault readers, *Das Kapital*); behind the tables of philosophy, partially inaccessible floor-to-ceiling shelves of American and British literature, essays, sociology, criticism, political science, and economic theory; on a folding table between the desk and picture window, biographies of military tacticians (Hannibal, Bismarck,

Talleyrand) and literary nonfiction (Didion, Lasch, Borges, some Baldwin); on the half-wall separating the study from the kitchen, dictionaries, atlases, western European history, and art history (Western and Eastern). That was the study, but there were also shelves and piles in the kitchen and dining room (mostly math and science), in his and my mother's bedroom (random bedside novels, some sociology); in the hallway underneath our family portraits on a caving plywood shelf (the complete *Encyclopædia Britannica*); in the basement (a whole library unto itself), in boxes in the garage (textbooks), on shelves in the laundry room (not sure), and in boxes in the attic (ditto). Sometimes, when Pappy was moving things around, there were books in the bathroom. The collection came to something between 10,000 and 15,000 volumes in total. All this, packed tight into a boxy single-story home—it put the laws of not only interior design but also physics to the test.

Coming up, I hadn't had the courage or the imagination to go against my neighborhood's grain, to be that kid who says: Screw it; I'm different. Where I lived, books were like kryptonite to niggas— they were terrified, allergic, broke out into rashes and hives. Charles Dickens was something that swung between your legs, not the author of *Martin Chuzzlewit*. You could get your ass kicked for name-dropping and using big words. Brothers weren't out to be poets or theoreticians; most of the time, they weren't even trying to be articulate—they talked with their hands (fists, daps, slaps, pounds, peace signs, jump shots, tabletop percussion) and yearned to be athletes and rappers, not scholars or gentlemen.

Like most teenagers, I was just trying to get by in the Darwinian landscape I found myself thrust into, maybe to get a little action on Friday night if I was lucky, and above all not to be considered a freak or a mark. The nail that sticks up gets hammered down. To survive, I drank in my community's mores, including its fear of learning, even as I capitulated to my father's seemingly eccentric will at home. After a hell of a lot of effort in both directions, by the time I was eighteen, I damn near had mastered the delicate balance of keeping it real and keeping Pappy satisfied at the same time.

And then, suddenly, everything got thrown in reverse when I started hanging with armchair philosophers and intellectual show-offs like Playboy. Different game, different rules—now it was more like: Come with a weak vocabulary, mispronounce Ingres or Descartes, stress the wrong syllable in *bathos* or *banal*, own up to never having heard of *Gravity's Rainbow* (You don't read Pynchon?), and you could get laughed at to your face. Up was down.

As always, the wrong diction got you pounced on and no one would come to your defense. But the definition of "wrong" had changed. Now it was the know-it-all, free as a schoolyard bully or bird of prey, who was tearing you to shreds, and there were enough wannabe Harold Blooms lurking around to shame any sympathetic philistines into submission. You could end up in incredibly humiliating positions if you got caught off guard. At first I couldn't believe what was happening—truly couldn't believe that at Georgetown everyone wanted to be the smartest person in the room—it was like I had driven through a black hole somewhere along Interstate 95 and entered into a parallel universe.

The embarrassing truth, then, is that I was ushered back toward books not by any noble epiphany or thirsty mind but by little more than peer pressure—ironically the same force that in high school drove me from them. But certain switches only flip in one direction, and soon I was reading for myself and myself alone. Back at home, free from Stacey, free from my neighborhood, free from the hip-hop demimonde at Georgetown, free from snobbish pretense, I began to hit Pappy's library in earnest. "You don't need anybody if you have books," Pappy used to say, and I was beginning to believe him. "Other than you, your mother, and your brother, these are my only friends, right here—and if you talk to them, son, you can talk to geniuses."

In the beginning, I set out to read whatever was most unlike me. I knew enough to do that. It was around this time that I met some of Pappy's old friends: Vladimir Nabokov and Humbert Humbert, F. Scott Fitzgerald and Jay Gatsby, Robert Graves and Emperor Claudius, Oscar Wilde and Dorian Gray. The vast walls of books in our cluttered little house became Borges's magical aleph and I found that if I looked the right way I could see the whole world.

Besides my family, the only people I saw regularly that summer were my old friend Sam and two young twin brothers named Shadik and Shadir, whom I had met through Sam and to whom I had become something like an older sibling. One evening, the four of us were at Sam's mother's house, up in his attic bedroom, listening to No Limit Records CDs and talking, his ten-year-old *Word Up!* magazine posters staring down at us from the sloped green ceiling. I was lying on the floor, flipping through a stack of Sam's old photographs. One of them in particular caught my eye. The picture is of Stacey and me. We are sitting at a metal and glass patio table in her grandmother's backyard. To judge from our clothing, it's one of those hybrid or crossover spring or fall days, part summer, part winter, where you can dress for whichever season you please and still be perfectly comfortable. Stacey is wearing Daisy Dukes shorts and a white wife-beater. Her hair is gathered back into a ponytail or bun. She has no makeup on and doesn't need any. I am sitting with my arm around her, dressed in baby blue velour sweatpants, a white T-shirt, and an open baby blue velour zip-up jacket. I have Tar Heel blue-and-white Nike Dunks on my feet and my hair is shaved low, almost bald. Both of us are staring straight into the camera like we were caught by surprise and only looked up at the very last moment.

Something struck me about this photo, and I lingered on it. Christ, I thought to myself the more I scrutinized the picture: I look like a giant-size toddler, ridiculous, like I've been swaddled in a pair of color-coordinated pajamas. I was in style, but whose style was I in? I looked like someone else. That's not me, I thought. And also, I wondered: Can a person who is dressed like this really ever be taken seriously? I was no longer so sure. I must have been staring at the picture hard right then because Sam motioned to it and asked, "Is it crazy seeing Stacey like that?"

Snatched from my thoughts, I looked up at him. "Huh? Oh, nah, man, it's crazy seeing *me* like that." I stuck the picture back into the stack.

Because I was busy or because I was already mentally long gone, the days that summer shuffled past like the pages of a magazine held to the wind. On one of my last, I went for a workout at Forest

Road Park, my old stomping grounds. It was nearing dusk, and the scent of honeysuckle infused the evening's humid breeze. The sky was a giant bowl of rainbow sherbet, all purples and oranges, and I had the main court to myself. I settled into my old routine: one thousand short-range jumpers, five hundred from the right elbow, five hundred from the left. When I finished, I felt a good kind of tired and sat down on the wooden bench behind the basket to get my breath. A rush of childhood memories came to life like mirages as I stared out over the deserted asphalt in front of me. Eventually, my mind wandered to RaShawn. I could see him grabbing on his crotch, sending a thin stream of saliva from the side of his mouth after slapping a finger roll into the parking lot; I could see him turning to me, handing over some singles for the Italian ice truck; I could see him pummeling that white boy in the Raiders jersey on the ground, after he was already down.

It was dark and the lightning bugs looking for mates and prey had started to glow when at last I got up off the bench. I took a few last shots before heading home. As I walked, I strung the ball back and forth through my legs with every step, trying to see if I could still make it all the way to my front porch like that. The last I heard of RaShawn, he had shot and killed a man. Murder was the case that they gave him.

The night before I left for school I took one last walk around the neighborhood with my mother. The two of us were quiet for a long time that night, comfortable like best friends in each other's presence and lost in our thoughts, when she turned to me and asked that I promise to do one thing for her.

"Will you promise you'll always stay true to yourself?"

"What do you mean, Mom?"

"Just be true to yourself, baby," she said, paraphrasing Polonius, "and as sure as the night follows the day, you can be false to no one—always remember that for me, honey, OK?"

"OK, I promise," I said, slipping my arm around her shoulders, and we were silent the rest of the way.

Before taking me back to Georgetown, Pappy, who had noticed the change in the way I was dressing and must have been eager to encourage it, took me to the mall at Bridgewater Commons and bought me several pairs of slacks, three or four shirts, and a couple of pairs of shoes and shoe trees. He didn't make a big fuss about it, just told me to try on what I liked and put his hand on my back, told me he was proud of me. When I got back home, I gathered together my old gear—Timberland boots, Sean John jeans and Iceberg sweats, oversized leather jackets, Polo and Enyce tops, North Face bubble coats—and asked my mother to give it all to Goodwill. I put away the gold chain that Stacey had bought for me in my dresser drawer and shut the drawer tight.

CHAPTER SEVEN

Beginning to See the Light

Returning to Georgetown was nothing like arriving that first year as a freshman. For one thing, the neighborhood no longer seemed so intimidating or foreign as it once had. It felt good and comfortable to be back. I knew my way around and had some restaurants to hit up, like Basil Thai on Wisconsin Avenue, where I first ate Thai food; or Heritage India, further up Wisconsin, where I first had Indian (just about everything was a first for me back then). Those old cobblestone streets outside the front gates and the town houses that stretch along them like rows of colorful dominoes reminded me of home this time—my new home, the place where after a year of awkward acclimation and progress that came in small fits and starts, I would begin now to create and craft myself anew and in all seriousness, to work on myself the way Nietzsche said an artist works on a canvas: meticulously and deliberately. Plus

I had friends to see and catch up with. Pup and Dee and I had gotten a high pick in the housing lottery the previous spring and we were going to be living together in Village A. Playboy, Rusty, Matt, and the rest of the Harbin crew were scattered nearby.

I had a new strategy for handling my class work, too. I had been talking with my friend Paul, who was a straight-A student seemingly without breaking a sweat, and I asked him what I could do to get better grades. "How can I get on your level?" I asked.

What he told me sounded simplistic, but he swore it was the secret to success: "Never miss class."

"That's it?" I said.

"I've never missed a class, and when I go I pay complete attention. That's it. If you just do those two things, I guarantee that you will see an improvement in your grades," he explained. Well, I'm going to do that, I thought.

I added a third component to the plan: I resolved to dress for class every day. Not merely put on street clothes instead of pajamas, but really get dressed, as if I were going to work or to an important meeting, as though class mattered. I was halfway through my nineteenth year now and aware for the first time in my life that being a teenager was not some permanent state, but rather just a phase that ought and must give way to adulthood. When I was a child, Pappy had always stressed to me the need to pay attention to my looks, not to primp or to be vain, but to be diligent about simple things like brushing my hair and cleaning my ears. He was impeccable in his own right, and I grew up watching him shine his own shoes and carefully fold and put away his suits. Like so many older blacks I've known, he placed a high premium on what was called "looking sharp." "How you dress, son, is the first and most immediate means you have of communicating with the world," he would often say. What his clothes had always said to me was that Pappy was a man. What the clothes my friends and I wore, the clothes we saw on BET and on the older guys at the park—the baseball caps and basketball jerseys, the big soft velvety sweats and the unlaced sneakers—what these clothes said, I became convinced by the end of freshman year, was that we had not yet grown up.

An appearance cryogenically frozen at age fifteen can be appealing for so many reasons, none more powerful than the fact that abusing sex, reeking of ignorance, using drugs, fighting, and flunking all appear more appropriate when—regardless of numerical age—you look like something less than an adult. I decided I was ready now to take responsibility as a man for my appearance. I would be vigilant about the messages I would let it send about me. I would never again show up to class dressed as if I were about to catch a touchdown or an alley-oop, or like I was about to stick up a 7-Eleven, like I had a Glock-9 tucked into my waistband. I would wear shoes to class and shirts and sweaters and trousers or jeans that fit. I would look like a man and not a kid. Some of my friends laughed at this sartorial one-eighty, it was so extreme, but I didn't care: If it is true that it feels good to look good, then it is equally true that it can feel gangsta to look gangsta and it can feel thugged-out to look thugged-out, or, on the other hand, it can feel smart to look smart. I wanted to feel smart.

My professors began to treat me differently, too, I noticed. It was as if I had stepped from beneath a shapeless burka or a paste-board mask and disclosed myself to them for the first time. They were seeing *me* and not just staring into a blank veil or a stereo-type, somewhere beneath which, presumably, *I* was concealed.

They looked me in the eye now, and I couldn't help but see that their body language was somehow different, too, somehow more agreeable when they spoke to me. I noticed myself responding to the way that they were responding to me and I began to participate more in the classroom and to meet with them outside of class. The gains I was seeing were exponential and compounding; they reinforced one another. At home, studying became easier and my papers got more coherent and nuanced. My confidence grew almost overnight. Paul was right; my grades shot up—I made the dean's list.

At the same time, I met a girl. A different kind of girl from any I'd ever met before. She was black like Pup, but also black like me. Her father was from Nigeria and her mother came from Italy. She was this tiny little girl—a full foot shorter than me and two years older—who had grown up in Manhattan, way uptown, and had just returned to Georgetown from a year spent in Tokyo. She had a funny Welsh name and spoke Dominican-style Spanish, lopping off *s*'s from the ends of words (*"bueno dia"*), as well as Italian and Japanese. She could pass for just about anything in the world other than white. In Japan, people thought she was Brazilian or, sometimes, when her hair was blown out, Indian. In the States, people assumed she was Dominican, which I did, too, when we met. In part, this was because of her bronze complexion, loose, curly locks, and thick Inwood accent. In part, it was just because she rolled around with a clique of Dominican chicks. She had gone to the Bronx High School of Science and used to want to be a chemist. Her passport had crazy stamps in it. She didn't know how to drive a car, but in New York she didn't need to—her feet worked fine— plus she knew the map of the subway system too well, could tell you when the F train was running on the C line and why and, depending on where you needed to go, whether you should stay toward the back of the train or move up to the front when getting off at West 4th Street. Needless to say, she took shit from no one. "At my size, I can't afford to," she would say with a laugh, revealing a beautiful, off-kilter smile.

She had a brown face, closer to my father's than my own, and was proud to define herself as black ("from the diaspora, yo!") but she also could use the kind of words I had started to use. The kind of words Pappy used. I didn't have to front around her—in fact, I realized, if I tried to talk to her the way I used to talk with Stacey, it would dead things from the jump—and she *liked* the way I dressed. She had transferred to Georgetown from U-Mass as a sophomore, spent junior year abroad, and now, as a senior, lived somewhere on the periphery of the black community. Her off-campus apartment was across the river, outside gossip's ambit. One night she and her girlfriends wanted to go dancing at George Washington. I had my parents' car with me that weekend and I offered to drive them (the one thing the suburban boy could do that the city girl couldn't!). As I pushed the car through traffic on M Street, I felt her small hands reach from the backseat and caress my shaved scalp. I don't know what she saw in me or how, but we became inseparable.

I would go over to her apartment in Alexandria and she would light the incense or scented oils she sometimes brought back from the Arab stores in Brooklyn or the sidewalk vendors in Greenwich Village. There was always food there—good food, chicken cutlets, lasagna, Cornish hen, main dishes and sides—she knew what she was doing, had been taking care of her father and younger siblings since she was twelve. While she cooked, I'd rifle through her CDs looking for music to play. Her collection looked nothing like mine; there was lots of Bob Marley and Stevie Wonder, Marvin Gaye and James Brown—shit I'd scarcely paid attention to before. The hip-hop that she did have was different, too: the Roots, Black Star, Dead Prez—the kind of rappers you just never hear in the 'hood, the kind of rappers I thought only white cats listened to and that my boy Sam used to call "Starbucks niggas." In high school my friends and I would have preferred to listen to hard white rappers than bump these black groups. "Throw your incense in the air and wave it all around like you just don't care!" I used to tease her when I came over. And yet, jokes aside, I found myself admiring the fact that this girl had her own taste and didn't just listen to whatever was on the radio and BET the way I did.

One day over winter break, Charles and Pup and I drove out to New York and met Betrys and some of her friends at a cheap Tex-Mex restaurant in the West Village called Burrito Loco or something like that. It was the first time I had seen her outside of Georgetown. Sitting there at the table with Charles and Pup, I felt so proud that I was with such an intelligent girl, a girl who was as comfortable discussing Buddhism as my friends at Union Catholic had been puffing "buddha." I sat there and realized that I *liked* smart girls—something I had not figured before, when I let my peers and certain entertainers talk me into thinking that a girl was the sum of appendages attached to a rear end and nothing else.

Being with Betrys changed my romantic worldview totally, a personal paradigm shift as powerful and irreversible as the Coper-

nican Revolution must have been for a diehard geocentrist. I
was learning for the first time to treat a woman with respect, to
approach her not as a sworn adversary, but as something more
than that. Far from feeling like a buster or a terry-cloth nigga or a
SUFLAN ("sucka-for-love-ass nigga") or a herb or whatever it was I
was *supposed* to feel like, I found that I actually wanted this, I was
more comfortable being like this. I didn't lie to Betrys and I didn't
worry that she would run game on me. I never wondered what she
was up to when she wasn't at my side the way I had with Stacey,
and this kind of peace of mind I found invaluable and stimulating—
stimulating because it freed me from distraction and permitted me
to focus on my schoolwork and to flourish. I forgot what it was like
always to feel sneaky or angry or jealous, constantly to be at war
with your girl. Now I just felt good—good in a childlike way, inno-
cently, in that way where you just like a girl and she likes you and
the mere fact of being in each other's presence is enough to make
you feel safe.

Of course this is the way that so many people experience dating
and love, and it is normal, but to me it was revelatory. I doubt that
Stacey or Ant have ever let themselves enjoy such tranquility, and
that is sad to me. But I am sure that they would want to. I imagine
that this is what all of my boys would choose were we not indoctri-
nated to preemptively sabotage our relationships with our girls,
and were our girls not trained to expect nothing better from us.

Still, I wasn't beyond seeking Charles's approval with regard
to the matter. On the drive home that night I asked him what he
thought about Betrys, did he think that she was hotter than Stacey,
something transparently insecure like that.

"Oh, nigga, please! Stop fishing for compliments," he said emphatically and to Pup's amusement, then added: "Seriously, that is a *woman*; Stacey is a bitch."

Apparently, not all bitches were the same for Charles anymore, and I just hadn't received the memo. Well, that kind of flexibility was OK with me now. I was no longer worried about maintaining some foolish consistency, and I was relieved to hear this confirmation and to hear it coming from his lips. Charles was changing and growing, too, I could see, which, I reminded myself, was really not the case for some of our other acquaintances—like Ant, who hadn't graduated high school or left the neighborhood, and who had offered a different view about Betrys to a mutual friend: "Aw, I heard that nigga Thomas went off to college and now he be running around with a boooooooouuugie bitch; that's waaaaaack!"

My parents, for their part, were ecstatic when they came down to D.C. and met Betrys. I could only imagine what agony they had suffered the previous four years, silently, at night, and in each other's confidence, as they braced themselves for the very worst every time I waltzed out of the house with their car keys or the phone rang and I wasn't there.

At the same time that my prefabricated notions of women were falling apart, so, too, were my assumptions about what I wanted to study and become over the next three years. I had entered school pre-declared as an economics major and took both micro- and macroeconomics my freshman year to equally disastrous effect. I hadn't really understood what economics was when I chose the field on my application. All I knew was that you could get a job at an investment bank with a degree in economics and a minor in, say, finance—whatever that was. And what I knew about investment banking was that the bonuses were outlandish and the consensus was that this was the safest and fastest way to get rich legally. Of course I can see now that I had very different first-job concerns than Pappy had back in 1959—I didn't worry about racial discrimination, I took for granted I could get decent work; I worried instead about how to amass and flaunt wealth. What shut Ant and anyone else up the summer before I left for school was the mere mention of owning a straight path to Wall Street, perhaps the only white-bread institution before which they all would bow their oppositional heads in quiet respect. "Oh, we've got a college nigga in the house now, so I'd better be on my best behavior," Ant would say at the park, and everyone would laugh. But no one would laugh (or they would stop laughing) if I replied that this college nigga was about to pull down a $100,000 bonus in just four short years.

The decision to study econ was as easy in its way for me as it had been for Pappy to take the crushing job at that insurance company. Economics gets you respect, I knew, because ultimately money is the only lingua franca. Of course, once I actually went to class, I found the subject matter so dry that I hated myself for having leaped blindly into it. But what were the alternatives? I had never considered the alternatives. Soon I would have to decide whether to stay with my decision—to stay in a field that I found uninspiring in the extreme but which others admired from a safe distance—or to switch majors completely. Playboy mentioned art history as a possible major I would enjoy, then he lost interest in school altogether and dropped out and we never spoke about it further. Pappy told me to study something honorable. My mother told me simply to study what made me happy. Charles told me to study econ and finance, as he was doing, and to fucking get paid and stop fretting. I heard them all out and continued to fret.

There is a basic philosophy requirement in the College of Arts and Sciences at Georgetown, and every student has to enroll in two introductory courses in the department, one of which is ethics. Like just about everybody else I knew, with the exception of Playboy, I had loose preconceptions about philosophy and took it for a joke or a chore. Pappy had always told me that I *should* read philosophy, but up to this point I never really had. When I arrived in Ethics 101, I wasn't sure what to expect, though the truth is that I didn't expect very much. The classroom was a large semicircular lecture hall in Healy, jam-packed with students who would never wish to be philosophers. The professor was a middle-aged woman with frizzy brown hair, the size of a ballerina, who had studied at Harvard under John Rawls and must have mentioned that fact a half-dozen times at minimum. But she was smart and engaging as well as immodest. She began class not by lecturing but by asking questions: What does it mean to live ethically? What is the purpose of ethics? And what does it mean to live "the good life"—that is, "to flourish"? These questions are silly until you allow yourself to take them seriously, which to my surprise I did from the start.

"Let's say there is a train coming full speed ahead and four people are standing on the tracks and they cannot see the train," the professor said. "You are on a bridge watching the scene unfold and next to you is one very obese man. You realize that if you just push the fatso over the bridge, you will surely sacrifice his life, but you will also stop the train. You would lose one life in exchange for four. What do you do? Does the good of the group supersede that of the individual? Is one life worth as much as many? Are some lives worth more than others? What are the individual's rights? Are such rights inalienable? Are there times when one must choose?"

What I liked most was that we were not being told to think *anything*; rather, we were being prodded to think *something*. These questions and others spurred me in a way that nothing in my economics classes ever had, and I found myself returning to them even outside of class. I found myself bending my thought back upon its source and subjecting my own life to a more rigorous examination than before. The way philosophy worked, it occurred to me at some point, was the exact opposite of the way the black, hip-hop-driven culture operated. Whereas the latter dealt strictly with the surfaces of things—possessions, poses, appearances, reactions—the former was nothing but the penetration of facades. The more I read in philosophy, the more I felt like that escaped slave from Plato's cave. I had been mistaking shadows for reality all along. The fact that this was such a sophomoric, clichéd revelation to come to in light of all my father's efforts to expose me to learning only illustrates the degree to which hip-hop culture—that invisible glue that stuck me with RaShawn—had placed a barrier between me and even the most universal aspects of intellectual life.

Still, moved as I was by philosophy, I had deep reservations about giving up on econ and a shot at Wall Street and all that that implied. Like Weber's hardworking Protestants and the rappers and ballers I had long idolized, I wanted the whole world to see and know that I was one of the elect.

The truth is that most white students I knew couldn't care less about the humanities or the liberal arts, the concept of a canonized Western literature and the idea of learning for learning's sake being as antiquated and, at the end of the day, irrelevant to them as it is to most Americans. For the black students, however, it seemed less that there was indifference to the humanities than there was open hostility to the idea of spending time in subjects like philosophy or art history or literature—this was seen as bizarre or foolish, perhaps even irresponsible and decadent. It was an outlook I could understand. Everything I had learned outside the house, from TV and in the 'hood, told me that book learning for edification was something only touched white kids could afford or want to do. This prejudice existed on every social level I encountered in the black community. On the one hand, the cats back home who didn't go to college, they weren't about to be impressed by the cogito or the importance of the Italian Renaissance in the progression of representational painting—not because they weren't smart, but simply because they didn't care. They don't give a damn about the noises in Raskolnikov's head or whether niggas can or cannot step in the same river twice. What does any of this have to do with their reality? Food for thought, you say? What Heraclitus eats don't make me shit, they retort.

What they can and do respect is that almighty dollar. Like the Notorious B.I.G., they love the dough. It seems perfectly acceptable to them that you would study finance or management or even marketing or cosmetology, or that you would go to law school (although *another* three years does seem a bit excessive). But it doesn't seem acceptable at all that you would contemplate the idea of personhood all day long and go to a fancy school just so that you can bring home a $35,000 paycheck and drive a used Toyota Camry (they can drive something hotter than that working at UPS, they point out, and they don't have to waste four years in college to do it). The idea that there is something to be had from education that somehow goes beyond material compensation is foreign and naïve to them—education is a means to an end and no end itself. They do not phrase it like this, but that is exactly what they mean when they say: You be on that bullshit.

That is what I saw in the black community back home. On the other hand, there were not nearly enough counterbalancing examples at the university to model myself on either. The overwhelming majority of the black students with status were either affirmative action recipients struggling mightily just to get by, or they were athletes on scholarship, or INROADS and Sponsors for Educational Opportunity all-stars charging full-speed ahead into high-powered corporate gigs. In the summers the latter went to intern at Goldman Sachs and McKinsey & Company while cramming for the LSAT on the side. They were gifted and elite, sure, but they were street smart, too, they were quick to point out; they had no time to gaze at a Caravaggio or wax romantic about dropping madeleines into teacups.

Some of these students would freely admit that they were anti-intellectuals: "I'm a hustler," a classmate said with pride, "it just so happens that school is my hustle." These black kids tended to want the same bourgeois material wealth that all the rappers and gangsters are dying trying to get; they just went about procuring it in a safer way. What drove them was the idea that they may one day buy back some of that legitimacy they mortgaged away over the years going to white schools and hitting the books. And how would they hope to do this? By going into entertainment law, for instance, and making seven figures representing actors and rappers. Or by going into commercial real-estate development or by working for a hedge fund or private-equity firm out in Connecticut and making so much paper that no one could begrudge them for it. Anything was possible, really—the sole unacceptable scenario was the one in which the material compensation would be less than ample enough to muffle all the player-hating.

In no way was I immune to such thinking. It is rare that you meet a black student who is, even at the best schools—especially at the best schools. We see images of athletes and rappers 24/7, but most of us simply have never seen a black person devoted to that other form of wealth, the life of the mind, and so we do not imagine that this is a feasible—let alone a luxurious—way to live. I had seen my father strive to live this way, to live his life inside books, and still, it struck me as an impossible fate for me to win. Part of me could not relinquish the desire to be a banker. Wall Street was such an obvious destination for a black kid steeped in hip-hop culture to want to end up at. The same machismo, the same allegiance to material wealth, the same condescension toward reflective thought, the me-myself-and-I worldview that was so prized in the street was equally exalted in the world of finance.

I used to lie awake at night, fantasizing about the day that, as a young hotshot director at Morgan Stanley or someplace like that, I would roll back to Plainfield, triumphantly, in a drop-top Modena or a tinted-up Geländewagen. I would be a black Caesar astride a six-figure chariot crammed full of booty and speeding toward Rome—victorious, chrome rims spinning, arm dangling out the window, gold Rolex Day-Date glistening in the sunlight, jealous jaws dropping in my glorious wake. I would show everyone I wasn't a sucker for having gone off to college. These images of hip-hop largesse were so vivid, I could even hear the CD I would be playing—Baby's "#1 Stunna." I was longing to ball.

For all my powers of projection, though, I failed to anticipate the extent to which daily exposure to serious ideas and methods of thinking would alter me. I didn't realize that once you leave home and see new and more complex things, you might just lose the desire to measure yourself by the old, provincial standards; they cease to motivate you even when you want them to; you set your eyes on new and higher (though they used to seem lower) sights. More and more, even as I tried, even as I willed myself to do it, I couldn't care what a Stacey or a Marion thought about me and my new lot in life, whether I would make more money than them or not. My points of reference had changed dramatically and definitively.

Concepts such as time and independence and freedom began to strike me on an intuitive level as more luxurious and precious than foreign cars and necklaces of gold. The thought that I could make a living *reading* or *thinking* was inspiring and even humbling. Of course, this is a kind of success that you cannot wear on your sleeve. You cannot "floss" the fruits of intellectual labor, however sweet, in the 'hood the way you floss a Range Rover on dubs. But I came to realize that I didn't really care about that, primarily because I no longer intended to be in the 'hood in the first place.

I didn't know where, but it had started to occur to me for the first time that there were other places I might want to go.

Anthony Perry, the St. Anthony phenom, was also at Georgetown in those days. He was two years ahead of me and I used to see him around, though not very often. He wasn't at the parties I went to, and neither were we in any of the same classes. From what I heard and could see, he played basketball and kept mainly to himself and his family. I think I recall he had children. He was not a huge campus personality. He was not loud and flashy like so many of his teammates (even the ones who had smaller names than his—especially the ones who had smaller names than his), but he stood out to me more so than the rest. He had a very New Jersey way of dressing, and his clothes—big T-shirts, big blue jeans draped over drooping Timberland tongues, leather Avirex jackets, knit skullies—reminded me of Michael's back in the day. He was quiet, even shy-seeming, with dark skin and huge innocent-looking eyes that probably had seen a lot, and which seemed to me deceptively out of place on his muscular, six-foot-three-inch frame.

I never said anything more than hello to him—and I doubt he had any recollection of those two awkward times we shared a court in Jersey City years ago, when he was considered the fourth best player in the country and I was not—but I liked Perry. I rooted for Perry. He gave the impression of being beyond the petty bullshit with which most of the other players were consumed. Maybe it was the St. Anthony humility and drive that Hurley instilled as a rule in each of his players. Or maybe I simply projected all of this on him and he wasn't like that at all. I don't know. I do know that things had not turned out for him the way everyone had assumed they would and that his once-brilliant NBA prospects were like a slow-burning sunset gradually fading to black. If *he* couldn't make it, I remember thinking, then I don't know what the rest of us had been doing devoting ourselves to such fickle dreams.

By the end of sophomore year, I declared my major in philosophy, and it felt like a tremendous weight had been lifted from my shoulders. I was trying to live as my mother had told me, no longer trying to be false or to be something other than myself—intellectually, athletically, sartorially, academically, or culturally speaking. Plus I was in love, and it was an innocent and good love, which, for the first time, I could share with my family. That summer, between sophomore and junior year, I spent every weekend with Betrys. She was still in D.C., but she would catch rides up to New Jersey with a girlfriend who was going to see her own boyfriend in Queens. I'd pick up Betrys at some pre-established point along the way— the Metropark parking lot or the Molly Pitcher rest stop, depending on her girlfriend's mood and inclination to venture from the Turnpike—and we'd drive back to my parents' house and throw hamburgers on the grill if it was early, or, if it was late, just hang out in the kitchen, talking with my parents and eating tortilla chips that we dipped in my mother's homemade salsa. Later, we'd excuse ourselves and go to my room and watch DVDs or talk about the books we were reading and what we wanted to be.

She wanted to put to use her considerable command of foreign languages, maybe get a JD and practice international law or work as a translator in a Japanese corporation or with the United Nations. I wanted to read and write and talk and think all day, so I supposed I wanted to be a philosopher or a writer, though I still didn't know exactly what that might mean. When I confessed this to her, she didn't laugh or bat an eye; she just encouraged me. We talked about making a life together. I would doze off dreaming about this life I had never before imagined could be mine but that I wanted now more than anything. In the morning we would have breakfast with my parents. She became like family.

During the week, while Betrys was in D.C. and my mother was at work, I would help Pappy with his business, addressing, stuffing, and sealing the thousands of envelopes that contained the fliers that hopefully would bring more students into our house. We spent more time with each other that summer than probably at any other juncture in our lives, and while we were stuffing and sealing those envelopes, we were also getting to know each other again, now as men. The two of us would lose all track of time in conversation and debate about literature and philosophy and the various ways in which one might go about trying to make a meaningful life.

One day, we had been talking about Oscar Wilde, which led to a discussion of the idea of art for art's sake, an idea I had defended and Pappy had dismissed. "Art, really, like everything else, must always be put to use for another purpose, and preferably for the purpose of teaching one how to live," Pappy said. I countered that to see art only as a tool is also to diminish it, to diminish the sense of joy that a work of art can elicit in relation to nothing other than itself. Pappy kind of raised his eyebrows at the word "joy" and told me to bring over the chessboard.

As I was removing the work from his desk and bringing the chessboard along with some sodas from the kitchen, he smiled and told me that he wanted me to know that he was very pleased ("pleased" would be the word he used, not "happy"; he rarely if ever would use that word) that I was reading good and serious books and deriving such satisfaction from what I read. I felt a kind of pride as he told me this. And then his expression changed and he looked out the window into the street and confided to me that, although he had read plenty of novels in his life, he felt he had never read a novel—or a book of any sort, for that matter—for *enjoyment*. He felt he couldn't afford to. He never had followed a narrative the way Wilde seemed to be in favor of doing or read a story simply because it was beautifully or skillfully crafted. "I have never read a story without a pen in hand, underlining," he said, "and not because I love to underline, son, but because I felt that I had to derive knowledge, practical knowledge, that I could then somehow try and marshal in my own life to make my own life somehow better. There was just too much that I didn't know, and nobody told me anything. I decided that everything I needed to know must be somewhere in these books, and if I just spent enough time with them, I could figure it out. So, no, I never did look at a book as just a piece of art."

Later, thinking back on this, I was for some reason reminded of all those St. Anthony players frantically playing a supposedly fun game whose joy, for them, was out of reach. The height of the stakes (perceived or real) rendered into a form of labor something from which others could simply derive pleasure. I realized that the only reason I was able to enjoy the books I read was precisely because Pappy *hadn't* been able to enjoy those same books when he was my age. I felt ashamed at the pride that had come over me when Pappy had complimented my learning, as it struck me that all this was profoundly unfair—an accident of time, little else—and that I must owe my father something more than simply being well read. I could also see that I owed him something other than the professional status and superficial material well-being so many of my friends and classmates were chasing after. I owed him something else entirely.

Pappy was very much on my mind later that summer when I bought and read a copy of *The Brothers Karamazov* (a very serious book of which I am not sure what Oscar Wilde would have thought). According to Borges, there is a special Islamic night, called the Night of Nights, in which the hidden doors to heaven are cast open wide and "the water in the water jars is sweeter than on other nights." It was something like this that I felt when I encountered Dostoyevsky for the first time.

I had decided a couple of months earlier that I had to read him, while sitting in the back of my Introduction to Modern Art class. The professor had put on the projector a slide of a small woodcut entitled "Two Men at a Table," by the German artist Erich Heckel, of the *Die Brücke* expressionist school. "This is a scene from 'The Grand Inquisitor' section of *The Brothers Karamazov*," the professor explained. "On the right is Ivan Karamazov, a metaphor for Intellect or Reason and Doubt, on the left, his brother Alyosha, a metaphor for Spirit or Faith. For those of you who have not read the Brothers K, Ivan has just delivered what many consider the single most damning refutation of Christianity in the history of ideas. It has been said that everything one needs to know about life is contained in this novel, so if you have not read it yet I highly suggest you go out and do so." Then he gave us some more background on Heckel and moved on. I copied into my notebook what the professor said about Dostoyevsky, and well after the slides had switched, the impression of that woodcut remained etched in my mind.

At first what drew me into Dostoyevsky—and against his will, I suppose, for he stood firmly with Alyosha—was this idea of the intellectual and of defiant reason, of the urgency of the struggle to be rational, of the pressing need to call into question received faiths by means of logical argumentation and critical thinking: in other words, the call to freedom. The superstitious Catholicism I had been spoon-fed for a decade and a half by drunken priests and well-intentioned nuns already had lost its grip on me. I didn't need Dostoyevsky to turn me into an atheist or agnostic—but I did need Ivan Fyodorovich to articulate for me thoughts that had been stirring inside of me and for which I hadn't previously had a vocabulary.

Men would prefer anything rather than be free—I had long seen evidence of this all around me, in Stacey and in Ant and also, of course, in myself. We were sheep and lemmings, the vast majority of us. Very few of us had anything like a real desire to be ourselves, to create ourselves. It was so much easier to receive direction from "above," and where I was from, above was the street, and the direction came from the rappers and thugs and hoes who were the grand inquisitors of the Real. They were the high priests and priestesses of hip-hop culture, which had become our religion and our opiate—really, our master, our new and terrible master. I had never known anyone my age and who looked like me who had read Dostoyevsky, but in his strange Russian world, I caught unmistakable glimpses of my own.

CHAPTER EIGHT

To a Worm in a Horseradish, the World Is a Horseradish

That fall, I moved into Kober Hall on Thirty-sixth and N Streets. I was still rooming with Pup and Dee, as well as Matt from Brooklyn, and a sophomore from New Rochelle named Achilles. Playboy had returned after having taken leave the previous semester and was living far off campus in a doorman building near Dupont Circle. He'd use our apartment as a home away from home between and after classes. There were always streams of people coming in and out, usually with sacks of sandwiches and sodas from Wisemiller's, the beloved deli across the street. Our place was very large. We'd received a high pick in the housing lottery again and taken a three-bedroom duplex with exposed brick walls and three separate balconies, each of which opened onto an interior courtyard below. One of the first things we did upon moving in was purchase an aboveground Jacuzzi and set it up in a half-hidden corner of the flat, sandwiched between a protruding brick wall and one of the balconies. The Jacuzzi, besides being exceedingly difficult to keep sanitary and pH-balanced, wasn't permitted in campus housing. Nor was it anything like lightweight, and I used to worry that one day it would crash through the floor into the apartment below or break apart and flood the entire living room.

I slept right above the Jacuzzi and beneath a south-facing window that I kept all the way open when the weather was warm. Early one gorgeous September morning I was jolted awake by a loud thud, which I reflexively took to be my overdue comeuppance for having been so foolish as to think I could get away with keeping an outdoor hot tub inside a dormitory living room. I hopped out of bed and rushed downstairs behind the brick wall, expecting the worst, only to find everything there to be intact and bone-dry. I was relieved but also somewhat puzzled as to what could have caused that thud, a noise so loud it sounded like a thunderclap outside my window or like the floor beneath me had given way. I began to think maybe it had all been a dream as I lurched back upstairs and into bed. No sooner had I fallen asleep than I was woken a second time, now by the ringing of my cell phone. I answered the phone in an early-morning haze and heard my mother's voice on the other end. "Honey, I'm sorry to wake you, but I wanted to tell you that an airplane has flown into the World Trade Center," she said.

"Huh?" I said, confused. "I mean, that's crazy, Mom, but did you really need to wake me up just to tell me that?" I mumbled into the phone, imagining some overambitious amateur clipping his Cessna by mistake.

"Well, we don't know if it was an accident or not. But I called because there are reports of smoke coming out of the Pentagon building, too."

I couldn't get back to sleep after that and so I slipped on some flip-flops and went downstairs to the TV. I can't remember if I was the first one there or if Matt and Achilles were already sitting on the couch watching the news. I remember more and more people came in the door and down the stairs, crowding around the screen. None of us spoke; we sat in silence, staring at what looked like the trailer for a slickly produced feature film on narcotizing repeat. Both towers were smoldering. People were leaping out of windows. I felt my stomach turn. Then, all of a sudden, the south tower just swallowed itself up whole—one minute it was there, the next it was not—and someone in the room said, Oh, Fuck! and covered his mouth, and tears welled in our eyes as we sat there staring at the television screen.

Later that morning or early afternoon, I tried my mother back at work. All of the circuits were busy and I was forced to give it up. I couldn't reach Betrys in Brooklyn, either. In a kind of collective daze, Playboy, my friend Josh, and I climbed up onto the building's rooftop, where, just over the Potomac, we could see a slanted brown-gray column of smoke spilling out of the Pentagon and rising in what seemed like slow motion up into the pristine azure sky. Gazing out across the shimmering blue water and into northern Virginia, it began to occur to me that what I had heard before almost certainly was an explosion.

Now the city was silent except for the sirens and helicopters that polluted the otherwise perfect late-summer air. The four of us sat up there on the roof, scanning the panorama of monuments, the Kennedy Center and the Jefferson Memorial, the Key Bridge and the

Capitol building, eyes darting this way and that, always drawn back to the blaze across the river. Someone got out a camera and took pictures, none of which would do the moment justice. After a while, none of us really wanting to be left alone, we went downstairs and out into the street together to try to get something to eat.

The city was deserted. There wasn't a solitary moving car on M Street—usually a rushing flood of traffic—save for the occasional black military Hummer or Metropolitan Police Department patroller. We walked in the middle of the road to a restaurant called Old Glory, which served big slabs of Southern-style ribs and which Pappy liked to frequent whenever he came to town. It was open and had a large TV turned to the news. We sat down and I can't remember what we ordered, probably sandwiches and beer.

Playboy, a guy of grand blanket statements ("capitalism is sick"; "I consume, therefore I am") and brooding and depressive thoughts on an ordinary day, began holding forth at the table right away. He had a lot to say about the many ways in which the world was presently dying and how Fukuyama suddenly seemed a hell of a lot less prescient than Huntington. History, far from being concluded, was yielding itself to an apocalyptic clash of civilizations for which the Western world had long been asking, that sort of thing. It was clear that Josh knew who Francis Fukuyama and Samuel P. Huntington were and was more or less acquainted with each man's respective lines of thought, though he professed degrees of cautious skepticism toward both. I had never heard of either of them before.

Feeling frustrated and powerless in general and ignorant and out of my league in this conversation in particular, as well as feeling a need to speak up and have a say, to leverage some kind of tenuous control over that day's events, I started saying whatever came to me. Really, I was just talking nonsense. "What we need to do," I said, "is to do it like John Travolta in that movie *Swordfish*—we gotta terrorize the terrorists. And while we're at it, we also oughtta deal with the China threat, too, because what they do to us is nothing but a form of economic terrorism, pure and simple." I used that phrase: "China threat." I had seen a copy of Bill Gertz's book by that same name on Pappy's shelf once and it was the first thing that crossed my mind that afternoon at Old Glory.

"The China threat?" Josh asked.

"Yeah, the China threat. People are not paying enough attention to that," I said.

"Can you even name the president of China?" Playboy asked.

"Mao Zedong?" I winced.

The conversation became ridiculous quickly. But this was the level at which all my old friends and classmates were accustomed to discussing the wider world, and I was only doing what I had grown up doing: talking shit. That is the way it works. Something happens and no one knows anything about it, or even tries to find out, yet everyone makes baseless claims, which we then proceed to wrap in the pretense of outrage or authority. The truth is that I was extremely confused about what was happening that day. Of course, the feeling wasn't mine alone by any stretch—the whole nation was caught unawares and forced to take a new look at a part of the world to which very few of us had ever paid serious attention, if any attention had been paid at all. Still, it is difficult to express the degree to which I was unprepared in matters of current events, foreign affairs, and the basic facets of twenty-first-century global reality.

I was especially ignorant for a student at a place like George-town and in comparison to my well-traveled and well-informed friends, people like Josh and Playboy. Until a much later age than either of them, I simply had never given much thought to what went on outside of my own very tight-knit demographic. I didn't watch the news, I watched Black Entertainment Television. For nineteen years, I had seldom ventured, mentally or physically, be-yond the guarded borders of the only patria I really knew or cared for, which was the nation of hip-hop. Neither had very many of my fellow countrymen. It was as though we lived behind the old Iron Curtain, inundated with propaganda, forbidden to leave. Eventually most of us developed something like Stockholm syndrome: We loved our captors and hated the world outside.

Even though I was trying to do better now, and trying hard, the adverse effects of a childhood and adolescence spent in this stul-tifying landscape lingered. It was not just complex but also basic what we lacked. No one I hung with in high school had a passport or the interest in obtaining one. We understood places like Latin America and the Middle East by way of the rappers we grew up listening to, jokers with monikers like Noreaga [*sic*] and Escobar, Kaddafi [*sic*] and Fatal Hussein—high school dropouts who spun glib yarns of boat rides to narco-states, of getting tied up by Colom-bians, of dictating microphones with iron fists.

We didn't think very hard about places like Europe or Asia or even Africa. I don't think that traveling anywhere beyond Barbados would have been considered keeping it very real where I was from. The farthest I had been was Tijuana. Charles had been, I think, to Puerto Rico. It's true that I knew some people here and there who looked like me and who were not like this—Betrys had lived in Japan and Pappy had been as far east as Moscow and all the way to Senegal and Mali; Sam's mother had been in Europe and many places besides—but I chalked this up to their exceptionalness and eccentricity more than anything else. In any event, the knowledge that they had been to these places and had seen from other angles failed to impress me. Even as I read more philosophy and literature, I retained a small and limited conception of the world around me—a fact that was made clear to me that surreal and eerily beautiful morning in September.

There is a brief passage in *Anna Karenina* in which a fast-rising general named Serpukhovskoy discusses romantic love, comparing its pursuit from the perspective of a young, ambitious man to the act of carrying a *fardeau,* or burden. It's as if you're carrying a burden while also having to do something with your hands, Serpukhovskoy reasons. Doing something with your hands becomes impossible unless you tie that burden to your back. Tying that burden to your back is marriage; lugging it around without marriage is to prevent yourself from getting anything accomplished. Of course, I was not married and I knew plenty of successful single students in college, but the fact that Betrys and I were in such a serious relationship, combined with the reality that she was now living in New York while I was in D.C., had the effect of freeing me from the relentless pursuit of sex—an overwhelming diversion that had governed my life and mind while I was with Stacey. Now, for the first time—because I wasn't trying to play Betrys the way Stacey and I had played each other—I was no longer available to other women, and the woman whom I loved was no longer

geographically available to me. I found myself able, finally, to subli-
mate all that loosed-up energy into intellectual momentum, and
this in turn allowed me to work harder than I ever had before.

Outside of the classroom, embarrassed by my evident ignorance, I was determined to turn myself into something like an in-
formed adult, though I was aware that I had a lot of ground to
make up quickly and I wasn't entirely sure where to start. One day
as I was studying in the library, Playboy, who never did work and
only read magazines, mentioned offhandedly that there was a well-
stocked periodicals archive on the second floor. "What do they
have that's any good?" I said, looking up from my books.

"Well, they've got a ton of *Harper's*."

"*Harper's*?" I said, snickering, thinking he was talking about the
women's fashion rag and ready to start clowning on him.

"Not *Harper's Bazaar*," he said preemptively. "It's a different
magazine—you'd probably like it." Then he went and found a copy
for me. He told me if I liked that, I'd probably like the *Atlantic*,
too. I took a long look at the cover, which seemed vaguely familiar,
and realized I had seen the magazine on Pappy's desk many times
before.

After that, I began to go to the library just to sift through the
stacks of old *Harper's* and *Atlantic* issues. I used to go alone and on
my free time. While Playboy and the others were out drinking and
trying to get laid, I spent many Friday and Saturday nights by myself
in the glass-backed reading room—me and the occasional janitor—
overlooking the Potomac and Rosslyn's bright lights, spooning
sugar into Styrofoam cups of coffee, making up for lost time.

Inside the classroom, I threw myself into philosophy. I gobbled
up the existentialists. In them I thought I could sense traces of my

father. As I delved into Nietzsche, I could make out Pappy's foot-prints. He had been here years before me, I was sure of it—little words and phrases, ideas I thought only he used, fragments, bits and pieces that he blended with his daily speech, which I had found so strange as a child—these were like clues now as I pursued him through the text. Like a detective, I began to map out swatches of intellectual terrain my father must have traveled as he attempted to make his way alone and make sense of that world he was forced to inhabit, a world that often must have struck him as excruciatingly absurd. I could envision Pappy's figure, alone and seated at his desk, scarcely older than me, rooming by himself because there weren't many other blacks to room with back then, coming across that passage in *On the Genealogy of Morals,* in which Nietzsche writes: "A strong and well-constituted man di-gests his experiences (deeds and misdeeds included) as he digests his meals, even when he has to swallow some tough morsels." I could see a line like that maybe providing Pappy a little comfort, another layer against the cold, and that made me as grateful to Nietzsche as to a friend.

But it wasn't only Pappy whom I found in these books. My old friends and I were there, too—everywhere I looked. Existentialism is the idea that existence precedes essence, which is only to say that our actions define us and we, in turn, are responsible for our actions. If, as Simone de Beauvoir believed, "one is not born a woman, but becomes one," then it began to seem to me that one is not born a gangsta or a thug or a pimp—or, for that matter, a wan-nabe gangsta or a wannabe thug or a wannabe pimp. If we learn to be who we are, then we choose to be one way instead of an-other. RaShawn *chose* to become a murderer; Antwan *chose* to be cruel to women; I *chose* to look up to and emulate them both. It all could have been otherwise. The existentialists, I realized, were continuing the conversation about freedom that Ivan began with Alyosha: What does being free imply, really? I remember coming upon the passage in *Being and Nothingness* in which Sartre observes that quintessential Parisian *garçon*, or waiter, from his table at the Café de Flore:

> His movement is quick and forward, a little too precise, a little too rapid. He comes toward the patrons with a step a little too quick. He bends forward a little too eagerly; his voice, his eyes express an interest a little too solicitous for the order of the customer. Finally there he returns, trying to imitate in his walk the inflexible stiffness of some kind of automaton while carrying his tray with the recklessness of a tight-rope-walker by putting it in a perpetually unstable, perpetually broken equilibrium which he perpetually re-establishes by a light movement of the arm and hand. All his behavior seems to us a game. He applies himself to chaining his movements as if they were mechanisms, the one regulating the other; his gestures and even his voice seem to be mechanisms; he gives himself the quickness and pitiless rapidity of things. He is playing, he is amusing himself. But what is he playing? We need not watch long before we can explain it: he is playing at *being* a waiter in a café.

I was reminded in those days of a boy I knew at Georgetown. His name was Will. Will came from New England. He had gone to a

good boarding school—in fact, to one of the best. He was on a tennis scholarship. He had pitch-dark skin, a slow easy gait, and a
wardrobe stuffed with Abercrombie & Fitch. He wore a navy blue
and red Boston Red Sox cap, flipped to the back. I don't think
there were very many black students at his boarding school in
New England, but at Georgetown, I can attest, he was popular in
black circles. He would walk through Red Square, stop at one of
the black-occupied benches, spot a friendly face or two and offer
his hand, dipping his shoulder, perhaps a little too low, as he leaned
into the dap. He would get drunk and blunted at night and talk
tough, sometimes maybe a little too tough. There was the time he
had a dispute with Achilles and he screamed some threats; perhaps he screamed them a little too loudly. There was also the time
at the bar in Foggy Bottom, when it was so crowded that Rusty
inadvertently bumped Will as he passed, and Will wheeled around,
fists clenched, shouting, "Yo, what the fuck you wanna do, white
boy?" His response, perhaps it was a little too angry. And then, just
before his graduation, Will was expelled from school.

"Will the tennis player—why was he expelled?" I asked a
friend.

"Dude bust into a white boy's dorm room with a gun!" my
friend replied.

In a real-life enactment of what the comedian Dave Chappelle
would call "when keeping it real goes wrong," Will got arrested by
the Metropolitan Police and kicked out of school. "He was dealing
marijuana," my friend told me, "and went looking for some money
he was owed." But Will had gone to prep school, I thought. Why
would he get involved in this mess? It doesn't make any sense.

The truth is he was playing. But what was he playing? I didn't need to reflect long before I could explain it: He was playing at *being* a black boy in the hip-hop era.

Will wasn't *essentially* a thug, or anything like that. Far from it. He became a thug—he *chose* that. And somewhere deep down inside, he must have known this wasn't him. This is what Sartre calls "bad faith," or living in bad faith. One *deceives* oneself into playing a role. It wasn't just Will, though, it was all of us who strove to keep it real. What were any of us if not meticulous little French waiters, our poses a smidgeon too rehearsed? Except for us, unlike Sartre's unfortunate *garçon*, our choices tended to lead to far more punishing environments than the Café de Flore.

My father was born in 1937, in Longview, Texas, the segregated South and the place where that strange fruit used to hang and swing from the trees in the lazy summer heat. His great-grandfather, a man named Shadrach Jones, was a slave in Louisiana. His grandmother, a woman named Cora McLemore, never had the right to vote. Though she owned some land, Cora also bore witness to Reconstruction, which meant, among other things, that sometimes she hid underneath the porch with her children and grandchildren, huddled and trembling, while the Ku Klux Klan raided the black side of town on horseback. These were the days when blacks would go to the emergency room at the hospital and repeatedly be passed over by whites—rich and poor, old and young—who came in behind them and got served first. You would see a black patient wait in the waiting room until he literally died from waiting, Pappy told me. Pappy himself was twenty-seven years old before the Civil Rights Act of 1964 forced his country to recognize him as a full citizen. His race, at least as much as his actions, defined him on the inside as well as on the outside.

For Sartre, of course, we all—every last one of us—are radically free, even Shadrach, for he had the choice, at least in theory, to revolt, to fight, to run away. He had the choice to commit suicide. He had the choice not to choose, to remain as he was. We are slaves, each of us, but only to our freedom, Sartre would have said. This idea reads well on the page. Perhaps it even is true on certain intellectual levels. I suspected, however, that on many other levels, on the level of lived experience for example, Will and I were far freer than Shadrach and Cora and Pappy and all those generations of blacks who came before us. That this was true seemed tough to deny, and the more I thought about it, the more the matter produced in me feelings that were not unlike guilt. Not the guilt you have when you do something wrong, but the guilt you have when you are given something you don't necessarily deserve or haven't earned by your own efforts.

Shortly before I was due to come home for Christmas break that year, I got an early Saturday morning phone call from Pappy. He tried to ask me how I was doing, but by his tone I could tell that he was not all right. What's going on, what's wrong? I asked him. He began to say what had happened at home the night before.

Clarence, who lived in the basement of the house, was coming back from his job at a law firm around ten or eleven p.m. As he parked his car in front of the driveway, a Fanwood Police Department patrol vehicle pulled up behind him, lights flashing, and two young officers of Irish and Italian stock hopped out. The police-men had been parked and waiting around the corner for who knows how long. They approached Clarence, who was still in his office clothes, and told him to stay right where he was. Because Fanwood is such a small town and because my brother had col-lected a lot of traffic violations in his day, he knew at least one of the officers by name, and the officer knew him as well.

"What's the problem, Officer?" Clarence said, lighting a ciga-rette and leaning against the side of his used silver Taurus.

"We have a warrant for your arrest here, Clarence," one of the officers taunted.

"What for?"

"Looks like you have an outstanding traffic ticket and you for-got to show up for court," the officer said.

"Ah, right, but there's been a misunderstanding," Clarence explained. "I did have a mandatory court appearance back on September 12, but with all the confusion over 9/11, government agencies shut down that day. The courts were closed, but the thing is that their computers were still up and running and so everyone with a date for the twelfth—me included—was automatically is-sued a bench warrant for their arrest. When court reopened on the thirteenth, notices were sent out recalling those bench warrants. I have that paperwork inside; I can go and get it for you."

"That's not necessary, you're going to have to come to the sta-tion and settle it there. But don't worry, you can spend the night," the officer said, and laughed.

"But there's no need to go to the station," Clarence said. "I have the paperwork right here—I'll go and get it." Clarence began to walk up the short driveway towards the garage door. The officers told him to stop. Clarence flicked his cigarette, kept walking and opened the garage door. As he began to step inside the garage, one of the officers grabbed him.

"Let me go," Clarence said, "I'm just going to get the paperwork, there's been a misunderstanding, I can show you."

"There's no misunderstanding," replied the officer.

"Fine, let me just call the station, then, and speak directly to a commanding officer," Clarence said reaching for his cell phone.

"Put your phone away now!" the officer shouted. Sensing that something was off and beginning to feel afraid, Clarence panicked and tried to close the garage door between him and the two po-licemen. Both officers stepped up. As my brother pulled down the door, one of the officers shoved him; as he stumbled, the other took his steel Maglite, cocked back his arm, and in one heavy swing, relieved Clarence of two front teeth. They scattered across the oil-stained floor like dropped Chiclets. My brother, who always has had a frightening tolerance for pain, screamed for them to get the fuck up off him. Refusing to fall, he struggled with both officers who were intent on wrestling him to the ground and they pushed him through the door separating the garage from the basement proper.

Pappy, who had been dozing in his bedroom, was awakened by the commotion directly beneath him and rushed downstairs. What he saw as he descended the staircase were two white policemen on top of his defenseless black son, now stretched on his back on the cold basement floor and fully within his own home. One offi-cer had Clarence pinned with a shin across the throat and was pounding his head against the cement floor; the other held his legs. Clarence, his mouth swollen, purple, and streaming blood, continued to rain curses on both of them.

"Now, you wait just a minute!" Pappy shouted as he entered. It is of the utmost importance to stress here that my father was sixty-five years old at the time—a senior citizen, with not only gray but also white hair—and he would have been dressed, like Clarence, in khaki pants or wool slacks, a dress shirt, a tie, glasses, and a sweater vest. But instead of calming down when an older man came in the room, one of those two heroes, the one who had Clarence by the legs, sprang up to his feet and drew his weapon.

"He put his gun in my face in my own goddamn home!" Pappy said into the phone, breathing hard enough that I became worried he would have a heart attack. "I've never broken the law in my life and this white boy pulls his gun on me."

I tried to calm my father over the phone, but there was too much going on, too much baggage, too much symbolism involved in the exchange he was describing.

"And do you know, son," Pappy said—in a tone of voice that I have not heard from him before or since, choking on his words—"I had a choice: I either watch these bastards beat my own son into the pavement or get killed slugging one of them and you and your mother are left in a hell of a fix ... Son, I'd rather die ..."

His voice broke, and for only the second time in my life, I heard my father cry. It is the most painful sound in the world, the sound of one's father's tears. Pappy's weeping lasted only a few seconds; he mastered himself as quickly as he had lost it. But those few seconds will echo through me for the rest of my life.

He began again, speaking calmly and under control. "Then your mother came downstairs, and she had the cordless phone in her hand; she had called the lawyer and the neighbors and they were calling the police station."

"How did it end?" I asked.

Pappy told me many things that boiled down to the following: They put Clarence in cuffs and took him to the station, his teeth stayed behind on the floor. As for the relevant paperwork detailing the change of date, it was right there on the nightstand, about fifteen feet away. (The town where the warrant originated later confirmed to the Fanwood police that the warrant had been issued erroneously.)

Was it foolish of Clarence to speed and get a ticket in the first place? Yes, it was. And it was probably also exceedingly bad judgment on his part to attempt to enter the house—regardless of whether there was proof inside of a change of date—after the policemen instructed him not to. I cannot dispute that. But try as hard as I can—and I have tried—I fail to see any way that this could have happened to any of our white neighbors, in their own homes and over an infraction so venial as a traffic ticket. It is simply unimaginable.

I don't think I will ever be rid of the visceral contempt and disdain I feel for the police. I have never felt safe around these undereducated and overly armed men whose job, supposedly, is to protect and serve. And I've never sought to delude myself out of seeing the racism that exists all around me. It is there for the seeing. And yet, be all of that as it may, this experience affected me primarily as a family tragedy, as a personal grief, not as a racial one. It never did hit me the way it hit Pappy. What fucked up my head for days was my awareness of Pappy's pain, that these two pigs had tracked their dirt and mud into our home, had desecrated my father's personal space and force-fed him fresh morsels of white-on-black injustice—just the kind of morsels he has been struggling his entire life to digest.

I hated these bastards not because I felt powerless against them—on the contrary, I felt superior to the brutes—I knew what they were like and what they went home to and what kind of rent they paid just as well as I knew that at the age of twenty and with tanned skin and wooly hair, I could already go places where these white men could not go. I hated these uniformed thugs not because they had beat my brother (though I hated them for that, too)—but because they had made my father the victim. This experience hurt and infuriated Clarence—and we are thankful that he did not go and get a gun and try to avenge himself on one of those cowards, as my mother and I feared he might—but he told me that it never diminished his self-confidence or led him to conclude that as a black man this must be it. The truth here, the hard, inequitable truth, is that Clarence and I actually *are* freer than Pappy. Though we experience racism—sometimes even violently—it simply fails to define us as it might have had we been born just two or three decades sooner. This struck me as both deeply tragic and extremely hopeful.

When I returned to school in January, Playboy had dropped out for the second and final time, was living somewhere near the Assemblée Nationale in Paris, and most of my other friends were studying abroad, from Buenos Aires to New Zealand. I now understood the importance of getting out of one's backyard, understood it well, but because I had received such low marks my first year, I couldn't afford any semesters off from Georgetown. For all intents and purposes, I had already taken my leave as a freshman, and so I stayed in D.C. trying to pull up my GPA as high as mathematically was still possible.

Charles didn't have these problems—he had a real talent for economics and had gotten himself into a prestigious exchange program at Cambridge. He was gone, too, and now I really felt left behind. To compensate, I got a passport of my own and arranged to visit him and Josh and Rusty in London that spring break. Having not yet completed Georgetown's basic foreign-language requirement, I also enrolled in a study-abroad program in France for the summer. I could have taken all the coursework I needed at Rutgers and saved myself a lot of student-loan debt in the process, but I had been living with a gnawing sense of unease that semester—a feeling my trip to London would only intensify—a kind of vague, undefined longing. A longing for what, I couldn't say. All I knew was that I had to go abroad and that it would cost me far more if I did not go.

Back at what seemed to me a very quiet Georgetown, I bided my time playing pickup basketball with Pup and endless hours of chess with my old roommate, Bryan. Academically, I pushed myself harder than ever. I met a very kind and serious philosopher from the Flemish-speaking side of Belgium, a Hegel scholar named Wilfried Ver Eecke. Dr. Ver Eecke—a balding man with thick accent and jowls, who looked anachronistically like a philosopher, always in a gray three-piece suit and almost always in his office, working—

took me under his wing and agreed to teach me *The Phenomenology of Spirit* on a one-on-one basis. He cautioned beforehand that it was, in his opinion, "probably the most difficult book in the world." As such, we agreed that we would focus our attention those months on one section in particular, a section I wanted badly to comprehend, a section Hegel called the Master-Slave Dialectic.

The Master-Slave Dialectic begins as a kind of imagined narrative or myth, which Hegel devised in order to explain on a highly abstract level how mere life, conscious life, might have made the staggering leap to become *self-conscious* life—or life that is aware of itself, subjective, "I." It develops into the story of what happens when two "I"s meet each other, when "the-I-that-is-I" encounters "the-I-that-is-other" and both attempt to assert themselves. It becomes the story of a life-and-death struggle, of a fight for *recognition*, of an unequal relationship that necessarily ensues.

To say that this is heavy stuff is the definition of understatement. I labored for months with Dr. Ver Eecke as my guide, trying to follow Hegel's elusive thought around the darkened Teutonic woods. The pursuit exhausted and challenged me in ways my teacher, a European man, could not understand. It challenged me emotionally. As a descendant of real slaves, my interest in the topic was instinctively more than academic—whereas Dr. Ver Eecke, through no fault of his own, felt it all in his head, through no fault of *my* own, I felt it in my bones. I felt, perhaps, a touch of ancestral shame. Above all, as a black student of philosophy at Georgetown, I felt profoundly alone. I had no one, not one black person I could talk to about what I was reading and thinking, about Hegel's concept of bondage in particular and about philosophy in general. I was the only black person in the department—student or faculty—and that was that. It is difficult to take a topic that hits home the way slavery does for blacks and twist it around in your mind theoretically, dispassionately, in the abstract, counterintuitively, but that is what I ended up having to do in the absence of anyone to speak with emotionally. This, though, I think, was ultimately for the better. I pried myself from my emotion and my history and let Hegel have his say. What he said turned me upside down.

For Hegel, it is actually *the slave* who comes out on top in the long run. In that initial life-and-death struggle, which sets the terms going forward, one "I" experiences what Hegel calls the "fear of death" and submits to the other. This "I" decides he "loves life" and concedes the fight. And this initially submissive consciousness, the slave consciousness, on pain of death, now serves the other's will and *works* for him. But it is through this very work that, eventually, he will come to surpass his master, Hegel reasons. On a basic level, this is so because it is the slave who masters objective reality, or nature. The slave takes the plants and animals and transforms them, through work, into meals; the slave transforms, with his hands, a tree into a table; the slave is most alive, becomes necessary, develops his spirit. The master, on the other hand, is parasitic, decadent, dependent. Without the slave's recognition, he is not even a master; without the slave's work, he cannot prosper.

I realized that Hegel was not really thinking about flesh-and-blood men and women here, nor was he probably concerned at all with the curious case of the American Negro. On the contrary, he was thinking about such abstractions as the progression of Mind through History toward the Absolute. The particular and the personal were of little consequence to him. He was contemplating societal evolution on an extremely grand scale, and he was seeing the Master-Slave Dialectic as on the verge of finding its resolution not through a man like Abraham Lincoln, but through a man like Napoléon Bonaparte, through the imperial implementation of constitutional monarchy in Europe. In other words, Hegel was thinking about men becoming citizens, but he was not thinking about black folk marching in Alabama.

Of course, it was hard for me to see how my great-great-grandfather, Shadrach—a man bought (or bred, who knows?) and legally owned by a certain Jones family of Louisiana, like a head of cattle—would not have taken exception to Hegel's reasoning here, were he given the opportunity and ability to read and rebut. Could a slave ever reach this kind of conclusion? I wondered. The idea struck me as either insane or a joke. And yet, the more I thought about it—that those who have been subjugated might actually over time be able to *gain* something from that subjugation—the more I struggled with this idea from my comfortable swivel chair, armed with the space and perspective I was fortunate enough to have been granted, the more I found it difficult to dismiss as simply false.

Meanwhile, hip-hop music remained my daily bread, same as always. I woke up to the beat, and it was on when I went to sleep at night. Even as I drifted further and further away from the culture and its priorities, the music I found to be much more difficult to escape. When Jay-Z's *The Blueprint* album dropped earlier that year, my roommates and I got our hands on a leaked copy a few weeks early and knocked it all day, every day for a month or two. I pumped it as hard or even harder than my friends did, listening to "Girls, Girls, Girls" so many times some of them asked me to stop. But by that point something basic had changed in my response to the music, and irreparably so. Whereas before I could whittle away entire afternoons with Charles, marveling at Jay-Z's perspicacity, at his cleverness with words or his unflinching insight into the human condition, I now found I could no longer get myself so worked up about it, as many of my friends—including my white friends—still could do. I listened to the music, and I listened to it a lot, but it became nearly impossible for me to be impressed with it on anything approaching a deeper level, to see rappers like Jay-Z and Nas and the Wu-Tang Clan, or even Mos Def and Talib Kweli, in the light I used to see them and so many still do: as something *more* than entertainers and petty egoists, as something akin to autodidact philosophers and thinkers, as role models and guides, as "black people CNN." I couldn't do it, not once I actually had some philosophy under my belt and was getting into the habit of thinking for and informing myself. In fact, the only thing that amazed me anymore was the idea that I had ever been so taken by these people in the past or had thought that they were somehow "kicking knowledge."

As the year wound down, I used to stop by at Bryan's apartment on Wisconsin just about every day. The place, a two-bedroom walk-up, with a futon, a TV, a PlayStation 2, and two turntables and a mixer in the living room, was small and sparse but always a good time. Bryan shared it with a recent Georgetown grad named Ted. As far as I could tell, Ted's life revolved around four things in no particular order: smoking ganja, playing chess, listening to rap, and studying for the LSAT. I didn't know anyone else who wanted to play chess as badly as Ted did, and over that we bonded. The three of us—Bryan, Ted, and I—used to hold down marathon sessions with Ted's rollout chessboard, which he bought at the U.S. Chess Center over in Dupont, and which Bryan would spread out over the cardboard box he used as a table on these occasions. Mainly, Ted and I played game after game and Bryan provided the soundtrack.

An infectious and indefatigable bedroom DJ, Bryan would light up a spliff or two or three and weave together hours-long mixes of Boot Camp Clik, Wu-Tang Clan, and Rawkus Records tracks from his booth in the corner. Over the course of these evenings, Bryan and Ted would say things to each other like: "Yo, God, what's the science?" They talked about "chessboxin'" and "the dun language" and "blessing poly sessions." In certain ways it seemed to me as if they were even more into hip-hop than my black friends were back home. But both of these two white boys were also strong students with significantly higher GPAs than mine. I wondered how they could compartmentalize their hip-hop experience so neatly, not let it interfere with their schoolwork or their careers, in a way that many of my black friends and I couldn't do. Bryan was from a background no more privileged than mine and certainly far less elite than Will's. How come he had never tried to smack a bitch or pack a gat? I asked myself. How come he didn't think that homework was wack or have a baby like Stacey did? How come he didn't have the same problems so many of us were having?

One of the main reasons, it dawned on me, is that too many blacks do not approach hip-hop *ironically*. Whites and other non-blacks like Bryan and Ted enjoy the very real pleasures of the music while avoiding the many pitfalls of the culture precisely because they listen with a sense of irony. For my black friends and me, there was nothing ironic about the business of keeping it real. Quite the opposite—this is what many of us were most sincere about.

When Bryan speaks of "keeping it thorough" or "holding it down" or "representing," it means something very different from what it means when someone like RaShawn says the same thing. In one case it is funny and innocuous, *metaphorical*; in another it is *literal*, terrifying, and homicidal. RaShawn, that childhood idol of mine, was not being ironic in the least when he bumped *The Chronic* in Forest Road Park and Dr. Dre rapped evocatively about letting the hollow-points pop. The violence and criminality of RaShawn's lifestyle went hand-in-hand with the rap lyrics he earnestly embraced, and with the miserable street culture those lyrics evoked in such garish detail. RaShawn had none of the necessary psychological detachment and emotional remove that Bryan could bring with him to the interaction. RaShawn saw himself in these songs, whereas Bryan simply came to appreciate hip-hop in the way that, say, someone not from India might come to appreciate yoga. Regardless of his enthusiasm for hip-hop, there could never be any question of whether Bryan might actually belong to the street culture that produced it. The truth is that he couldn't, and no one would ever expect him to—hence the irony of his adoption of this peculiar language and set of manners. No, Bryan was into hip-hop, I realized, but he wasn't of it; sadly, RaShawn was of it even more than he was into it.

Without intending to, I had begun to listen to hip-hop with the ears of a stranger. I first realized this in a car coming back from the

Jersey Shore with Charles and Betrys and a friend of Betrys's from Tokyo named Jenny. The four of us were in good spirits after having spent the afternoon sipping cold beers on the porch of my friend Chris's beach house and lying on the sand. Chris was two years behind me at Georgetown and we had become friends that summer in France, where we both took language courses in Tours. The girls and Charles and I had taken our leave of Chris, and I was inching along the Parkway, stuck in the crush of Sunday evening beach traffic, with Betrys up front next to me, and Charles and Jenny in the back. Jay-Z's *Reasonable Doubt* played on the stereo and we all were quiet, listening to the rapper who called himself "Jay-Hovah" as if to the Sermon on the Mount.

This had been one of my favorite albums as a teenager. I played it so much in high school on my Walkman and in my bedroom that I eventually snapped the tape in the cassette. This afternoon the record still sounded good to me in the way that only a record that embodies all the mixed-up hopes, dreams, emotions, lust, swagger, naïveté, arrogance, innocence, and aspiration of a specific, irreproducible youthful moment can sound good. Which is to say, it had the sweet sound of nostalgia in it. But when I heard it now, heard "the god MC" narrate the glories of street life and state so matter-of-factly that "all us blacks got is sports and entertainment" and "thievin'," and when I heard him boast about his underworld ties and how the high price of leather and fur had him "deeper than ever" in the drug game, I must have kind of chuckled or something. It seemed to me to be silly on its face now.

The fact that until that moment I had been nodding my head along in solemnity also struck me as, well, ironic. What did Jay-Z's gritty take have to do with our present reality? Charles had just come home from half a year spent in the company of Cambridge dons and was starting a lofty summer internship on the trading floor at J. P. Morgan, Betrys and Jenny could read kanji, for heaven's sake, and I had just returned from a two-month stay in the *hôtel particulier* of an old French aristocrat who cooked steak dinners for me. Of the five of us that day, Jenny and Chris were not black; Charles and Betrys and I were. I could see very little distinction among any of our lives right then: We all had prospects beyond sports or thievin' or drug hustling. Yet somehow for Charles and Betrys and me, that was what was supposedly "real."

All of this was going through my head when, with my foot on the brake, I looked over at Betrys and made a sarcastic comment at the Jigga Man's expense. He had rapped something about consuming fine wines and issuing vintage flows.

"I bet if you blindfolded Jay-Z, he couldn't tell the difference between a red and a white," I said. Betrys and Jenny laughed, but Charles got annoyed with me as though I had insulted a friend.

"Why couldn't he? What, you have to have lived in France to be able to do that?" he said.

"Oh, come on, man, just picture Jay-Z in a cave in Vouvray or Rheims, doing a tasting . . ." The girls continued to laugh.

"I don't see what's so funny about that," he said.

"Huh?" I said, letting the question of Jay-Z's interest in viticulture drop, not understanding why it had ever become so serious in the first place. I kind of just looked back at my friend through the rearview in disbelief. Maybe he was just playing devil's advocate with me, arguing for the sake of arguing, but I took his dissatisfaction at face value. I simply couldn't see how any of us could claim to relate to Jay-Z in earnest anymore; doing so now seemed a sort of bad faith because who Jay-Z spoke for wasn't who we were. But for Charles there seemed to be nothing ironic about Jay-Z or the life he represented and put forth to the world as our black reality. Though Charles certainly couldn't be considered to live in this reality anymore, it somehow remained sacrosanct to him nonetheless. Whatever irony there may have been here, it was lost on my friend, same as I imagine it must be lost on other highly successful hip-hop generation black men like Jay-Z and Russell Simmons—men who make their incredible fortunes legally and are a very safe distance from the street life they so sincerely revere. For extremely smart and talented men like Charles (and like Jay-Z and Russell Simmons, too), perhaps this is not such a big deal. Certainly Charles was in no more danger of going out like RaShawn than I was. But Charles was a real oddity—a kind of cultural centaur, half 'hood superstar and half Cambridge boy—and the thing I started to realize as I contemplated my friend's dexterous ability to both thrive wildly and keep it real was that I have met a hell of a lot more RaShawns in my life than Charleses.

I wished I could explain all this to him, what I was thinking, but it wouldn't have been any use. For Charles, it came down as it always did to an unstated question of allegiance, and one ought to be loyal above all else, including being truthful: to family, to other blacks, to one's past, even to the street. He wouldn't budge.

I began to sense that, being black, there were just things I wasn't *allowed* to say about my culture or my tribe. This thought had not occurred to me before. The traffic on the Parkway hardly budged for miles and it was a very long drive home that night. I don't think Charles and I saw each other again the rest of the summer.

CHAPTER NINE

Every Secret Loses Its Force

An atmosphere of siege hung over Washington at the start of my senior year at Georgetown. Nerves were still raw from the previous September and the fear of terrorism was palpable wherever you went. The country was at war in one Muslim country and it looked ever more likely that we would be at war in a second one, too. Osama bin Laden's trail had long gone cold somewhere in the mountains between Afghanistan and Pakistan, and his organization, Al-Qaeda, released videotaped threats and taunts with seeming impunity. People, old and young, white and black, were on edge, to put it mildly. And then the bodies started dropping.

For twenty-two days straight, all up and down Interstate 95, a sniper lurked, picking off victims apparently at random. No one was spared: a thirteen-year-old student arriving at middle school, a seventy-two-year-old retired carpenter walking up Georgia Avenue, a bus driver taking a stretch on the steps of his bus, a woman vacuuming her car, a landscaper mowing a lawn, a part-time taxi driver fueling up, a Home Depot shopper walking to her car, a babysitter reading a book on a bench, a man pumping gas at a Sunoco station, a man pumping gas at an Exxon station, a diner coming out of a Ponderosa steakhouse, a woman unloading groceries into her car, another woman unloading shopping bags into her minivan. All were shot from a distance, each with a single bullet, ten fatally so.

For weeks, all the police could say was that they believed the killer was driving an unmarked white van. You don't realize how many unmarked white vans there are in a major metropolitan area until you begin to believe that they are shooting at you. Unmarked white vans are like taxi cabs or Toyota Camrys—they're everywhere. I remember scuttling back and forth to class that October, looking over my shoulder, spotting a white painter's van parked somewhere down Prospect Street, and feeling my heartbeat quicken and my muscles tense as I half braced myself to get clapped in the back. Rusty, Josh, and I were sharing an apartment together on M and Bank Streets, with a big picture window overlooking the bustle of M Street and the Key Bridge in the distance. We were all bothered enough that we kept the shades drawn when we got home from class and glued ourselves to the local news, which often was bizarre. All over the Beltway, from Maryland to Virginia, you would see these images of motorists at gas stations, ducking and hiding while fueling their cars, poking their heads up from behind their trunks, glancing around for ghastly white vans, anxiously awaiting either the pop of the pump or the gat, whichever came first. The world, it seemed, was an unhinged and inhospitable place. Even after John Allen Muhammad and Lee Malvo were apprehended and exposed as blue Chevy Caprice drivers, it was a long time before I stopped counting all the white vans around me.

In spite of all this—or perhaps because of it—I felt a heightened vigor and thirst for life, of a level which I had not previously known. I really was aware, maybe for the first time, that I was alive, and, more than that, that I was not just alive but even living well. I was aware, when I walked, of the ground beneath my feet. Fresh from a summer spent mostly in France, I was aware that I had traveled a very long way from Unisex Hair Creationz, Forest Road Park, and Union Catholic. Those two short months in another country and another language had recalibrated my inner compass in ways that lingered with me. I was aware now that I had floated in the Mediterranean and sipped an *orange pressée* at the Closerie des Lilas and seen the sun set in Montmartre. I was aware, above all, and at long last, that the world was a broad and grand place and that I was equal to and worthy of my surroundings wherever I went. I was also aware that no one, white or black, could take that from me. I cannot overstate the importance of this realization.

In class, I was engrossed in the philosophy of Martin Heidegger. Out of class, I spent a lot of hours with Josh at the Barnes & Noble down on M Street, in the second-floor coffee shop, exploiting the generous reading policy, trying to absorb everything and anything I could get my hands on and poring over piles of magazines, anything from *Wallpaper** and *Vanity Fair* to *The Economist* and *Harper's*. It was in the November 2002 issue of this last that I happened on an article published under the subtitle "The Disappearance of the Black Individual," written by a black professor at Stanford named Shelby Steele. I hadn't heard of Steele, but I flipped to his article and began reading, and what I read, to my surprise, seemed to be speaking to me directly, dovetailing with some of the very dense Heidegger I was struggling through and distilling all that German thought, oddly, into something distinctly black and extremely personal.

I was trying very hard in those days—with the whipped-up fervor of the redeemed or recently converted—to live out with seriousness what Socrates had called the examined life. By the time I encountered Heidegger at Georgetown, I felt, if not like a real philosopher, then at least like I was beginning to be an honest student of the subject. I was on the scent of philosophizing now and I felt that, with enough hard work and time, I could one day be a philosopher in the only sense of the word that mattered to my father—in the sense that I might ask serious questions and then use the answers to try to live a better life. My adherence to Pappy's interpretation of philosophy led me to take whatever it was that I was reading much more seriously outside of the classroom than even inside it. And this is probably why I was never able to become very interested in analytic philosophy, that cloistered, academic esotery that denies the possibility of deeper truth, and which all too often has given up asking the question "How ought I live?" "How ought I live?" was really the only question I wanted to find an answer to, and I looked for it in everything I read.

The more I read, the more I noticed that Pappy's problem of running with donkeys and mules had become a recurring theme in the literature I consumed: The psychologists spoke of "the group," Nietzsche of "the herd," and Sartre said, simply, "Hell is other people." Nowhere, though, did I find the issue described so forcefully as in Heidegger's exploration of the "They." The basic idea is this: Since we all live in the company of other people, all individual human life ("being-there") is really social life ("being-with"). And this social life ("being-with-one-another") is defined by "distantiality"—an individual's endless concern with the *distance* of his own practices from the accepted practices of his community. Distantiality is something like the pressure people feel to *keep it real*, a pressure that puts all of us, as individuals, in a state of constant *subjection* to others, the They, who decide what is and is not acceptable in the community. When we try to determine who They are, we realize that They are *nobody*. They are not *definite*. Like agents in *The Matrix*, anyone in the group can be the They at any given time and the They is never anyone in particular. It is generic and, as a result, extremely difficult to pin down or challenge. And this is decisive: The sheer inconspicuousness of the domination—most of the time we don't even notice it—is what makes it so powerful. Heidegger calls this invisible influence the "dictatorship of the They" and it is precisely what Pappy was afraid of when he wondered aloud about locking his thoroughbred away.

I was thinking about Heidegger when I began reading Shelby Steele. Early in the *Harper's* essay, he summarizes a movie seen in his youth that has left a deep impression on him. The movie is *Paris Blues,* and the setting is early 1960s Paris. The action takes place in the smoky Left Bank cafés and basement nightclubs for which the city was famous in the Jazz Age. One of the four main characters is a man named Eddie, played by Sidney Poitier, who begins to undergo a deep internal conflict. Eddie has fled to Paris, like so many black American artists and intellectuals of his generation, to develop his musical gifts and to escape the stifling racism that haunts him back home. At first he is very happy for having made his move. A romance ensues with a beautiful black teacher named Connie, played by Diahann Carroll. Things go well and Eddie becomes a staunch proponent of expatriation as a way of life for the black American. While he's walking down the Champs-Elysées, it occurs to Eddie that he never wants to leave Paris. Paris for Eddie is synonymous with freedom, America with hell. But Connie has not expatriated to Paris, she has come on vacation, and with her she brings news of the Civil Rights movement that is unfolding at home. As Eddie and Connie fall deeper in love, Connie makes it increasingly clear to Eddie that their future together lies not in Europe, but in the struggle going on in America. In one fell swoop, Connie presents Eddie with the very thing he is in flight from: the idea that group identity takes precedence over individual freedom.

Eddie rejects this idea and, as Steele sees it, it would be simplistic of us to write off his reaction as somehow ignoble or ungenerous. For Eddie already has won in Paris the very freedom that blacks in the States lack and are fighting for. And he has this freedom as the direct result of having understood himself not as a member of any racial group but as an individual who is free to make his own choices. Even if blacks were to win the fight back home, true freedom still would mean that individuals would have to make their own choices. Why, then, should Eddie wish to leave Paris for the brutalities of America, Steele wonders. The movie ends inconclusively, with Eddie promising to join Connie back in the

States, but staying behind to arrange his affairs in Paris as her train pulls out of the station.

As I read, I was enthralled. I could see Heidegger in concrete terms through Steele, who now shifted his exploration of the dilemma away from the movies and into the historical record. Eddie's unresolved fictional dilemma achieved its real-life denouement in the artistic life of James Baldwin, who in the 1940s swapped tenement living in Harlem for bohemian poverty in Paris and Switzerland, where he found—or better yet, created—himself as a writer. In Europe, crucially, he was able to come to terms with himself—as a Negro, as a homosexual, as an artist, as an American, as an unloved son—in ways that he could not while he was at home. James Baldwin became a huge success in Europe and it was clear to everyone including himself that his escape from America was instrumental in this, both artistically and existentially.

And then in 1957 James Baldwin returned to America to join the Civil Rights movement and became once again not an individual who happened to be black, but a black American who was fully accountable to his group. This move weakened him as an artist, in Steele's view. This opinion, I knew, was debatable. What was less disputable, though, was the idea that the work Baldwin began producing upon his return and continued to produce for the rest of his life was pretty much exactly what the group wanted him to produce. He put his own talents and abilities—he put *himself*—in service of the group, and he never again enjoyed the kind of freedom he had won in those early years of discovery and experimentation in Paris.

As I read and thought about all this, I was haunted by one especially poetic sentence in Heidegger: "Overnight . . . Everything gained by a struggle becomes just something to be manipulated. . . . Every secret loses its force." The more the individual feels a need to keep it real, the more he is pushed toward "averageness" and a "leveling down" of all possibilities and varieties of being. The They separates the individual from himself. For Heidegger and Steele, the stifling of individual freedom by the collective will of the group poses a grave existential threat in itself. It is not a threat that is restricted to the black community by any means. Quite the opposite, it is characteristic of all communities and herds.

For Heidegger all Others represented a kind of leveling down and loss of self, but for me, some Others seemed *better* than other Others. As I thought of James Baldwin and Eddie and of my own parents' commitment to the Civil Rights movement, as black-and-white stills of Martin Luther King and Malcolm X and Selma and Central High flitted through my mind's eye, I couldn't help but feel that it was one thing to give yourself over to the service of a worthy and moral cause, to lose yourself in your group when your group is engaged, against all odds, in a battle for its very survival. It was one thing to keep it real with your group when your group's reality is that their children are being firebombed in church and hosed down in the streets, torn apart by German shepherds and broken up by billy clubs. That was a sacrifice of personal freedom that I could understand. But it was something else entirely to realize that you have lost yourself for absolutely nothing, that you have been manipulated and dictated by a posture, an attitude, a pose, by BET, Trick Daddy, Puff Daddy, and the Junior Mafia.

As I thought of myself and my friends, all I could see was that the They into which we had been folded growing up had no dignity to it, no honor; it was shameful and misguided, an empty promise at best, a cruel hoax at worst. I sat for a while just staring at the magazine spread on the table before me, unable to take in anything else, lost in thought. Josh finally broke the silence, said he needed to leave, to go get dinner. We put our magazines back on the shelves and made our way out onto M Street and into the cold late-autumn air.

When I had opened Steele's article that afternoon, James Baldwin, like Ernest J. Gaines and Edward P. Jones and so many others I am reluctant to admit, was only a name to me, someone Pappy had told me I ought to read, and someone I had yet to sit down with and spend time getting to know. By the time I closed the magazine, it was clear to me that James Baldwin was someone I would eventually have to cross paths and come to terms with, and I would need to prepare myself for the day that I would do that. And even though I had no idea how this might come about, it was also clear to me that France was somewhere I would need to return to. My devils, whatever they were, were not the same as Eddie's or James's, not the same at all, but I did have devils of my own and it was obvious to me that I would have to shed them if I was ever going to become myself and learn to be free.

What I had only begun to suspect in my gut over the previous summer in Tours I was now certain of that afternoon in Barnes & Noble: Being serious about realizing myself as an individual required nothing less than my leaving for an extended period of time the black culture I had grown up in, severing myself completely from the miasmic influence of my group. I had to cease "being-with" my culture in order to become unaccountable to it. This was something I had already begun to do in fits and starts but couldn't do more than halfway while remaining at home.

At the same time, my long-distance relationship with Betrys, for two years an oasis in a desert of incoherence and distraction and the source of so much calm and inspiration, was beginning to fail. Absence, though it makes the heart grow fonder, can also turn two people into strangers. To my horror, the latter was now happening to us. Or, more likely, I was becoming a stranger to Betrys. I do not know precisely when everything began to change, but I do know that I was certainly too self-involved and too young to be able to give back to her all that she was giving me. When we saw each other now, we fought—something we never used to do—and when I came home for Christmas that year I rashly broke up with her. Our relationship had fallen apart and neither of us was taking it very well. I was riddled with guilt but unable to take back what I had let myself say. The whole thing seemed like a very bad dream I kept thinking I would wake from. What made it more difficult was the fact that we did not have a clean split: There remained too many tortured phone calls and tearful visits and framed pictures that never came down from the desk. Still, a barrier had been crossed. Even as I stressed over Betrys, I knew that I was no longer tethered to New York City or obligated to move there when I grad-uated, and this, I realized, was my chance. I began to research jobs in France and prepare my parents for the reality that, against their hopes, I would not be getting an advanced degree anytime soon.

As the weather turned warm and Copley Lawn filled again with freshly tanned bodies spread out on colorful blankets, I published an article in the black-run campus newspaper, *The Fire This Time*. I had never written an article before, but one of the paper's editors asked me for a submission and after a lot of thought, I decided to write something honest about an experience that had frustrated me. Earlier in the year, after having searched in vain for a chess club to join, Bryan and I, along with Ted and later Josh, decided to found our own. We collected about seventy signatures and some donations for pieces, boards, and clocks, secured classroom space, and began to meet every week and play round-robin tournaments. We became the Georgetown University Chess Club. I was glad to be able to do this, to find a good number of like-minded students and bring them all together over chess, the game that bonded me to Pappy.

All my satisfaction notwithstanding, though, I couldn't help but notice week in and week out that, of all the students who expressed even a fleeting interest in the club, only one happened to be black (and I'm almost positive that he was in fact Haitian). Why, I began to wonder to myself at these meetings, were so many Caucasians, Asians, Arabs, Indians, Muslims, gentiles, and Jews—boys and girls of all kinds of ethnic, economic, and racial makeup— interested in our club but black students were not? Was it because there were so few black students on campus to draw from? I wondered. Blacks were a minority at Georgetown as they are at most schools, but the correct white/black ratio was not 69:1. It couldn't be that, I realized. Then was it because chess somehow wasn't "real" and couldn't possibly appeal to "real" blacks? I didn't think that could be it, either. I had put in lots of hours lurking at the public tables over in Dupont Circle, which are dominated by black men, many of whom appear to come from the 'hood and are self-schooled and, for a few dollars, capable of taking out the occasional Russian master who wanders over in search of some action. I had also seen black men run outdoor chess from Washington Square Park in New York City all the way to the concrete tables outside Magic Johnson's Starbucks in Englewood, California. It may not be dominoes or spades, but chess is plenty appealing to blacks, at least in certain environments. Besides, I knew other black students right here who had a working knowledge of the game and played it on occasion. Why didn't they ever come out? The answer, I was sure, lay elsewhere.

In my article I decided to make the case that what I was seeing in my experience with the chess club was really just another example of the same larger phenomenon I had been involved with and observing over and over again since I was a child: Wherever there is a group of blacks that is surrounded by a group of non-blacks, there can also be found a profound unawareness and incuriosity—even an antagonism—toward anything not deemed authentically black, the definition of which, of course, is always shrinking. The problem here, as far as I could see, was more complex than chess simply not being a black game or my black classmates being uninterested in joining student organizations and clubs. Neither was the case. Black students came out in droves to join organizations like the Black Student Association, the Caribbean Culture Club, and the black dance troupes, but they did not join in any real numbers, if at all, the Skeptics Society or any of the non-black campus newspapers—or the chess club.

By my lights, this was evidence of the group, of Heidegger's They, partitioning what was black from what was white and of individual black students intuiting the boundaries and obediently staying inside them. Which was why in other environments, environments where most if not all people are black, like that corner of the park at Dupont Circle or even Pappy's segregated South, chess could be played out in the open and no one would think twice about it. This is what I argued. I made my case and called on my black classmates to integrate themselves more forcefully into the broader campus community and to stop self-segregating in the same old all-black groups and clubs. To do so would be the only way that we would cease being what we always complained of being: outsiders.

When I finished writing the piece, I read it and reread it several times over. I felt confident in my positions, but also a little nervous about the reception the work would receive. I sensed that I was again saying something I wasn't allowed or supposed to say. Before submitting the article, I asked Josh to take a look and tell me what he thought. "This column," he said, "is going to ruffle some feathers, man!"

"Good," I said, and I hoped that he was right. I let the editor publish my personal e-mail address beneath my byline, that was how badly I wanted to spark the debate. The editor, when she read the column, told me it was good and that she was even tempted to agree with me, here and there. In any event, she accepted it without making any changes, and it was out of my hands.

Several weeks passed, the article was published, I readied myself for the backlash I was sure would come. I waited and I waited. The silence, ultimately, was deafening. "Well, the thing is," the editor told me when I asked her about it, "the thing is that not so many black students actually read this newspaper."

By then, I was very much ready to leave Georgetown. One afternoon I was walking with a friend into Wisemiller's to get some food when I ran into the short-haired girl I had danced with at that track party all the way back at the beginning of my freshman year. That seemed like eons ago now, and without wishing to be impolite, I felt that the last thing I wanted when I saw her approach was to have to talk to her and possibly even explain myself while I was at it. "Hey," she said.

"Hi," I said.

"Well, are you going to be graduating?"

"Am I going to be graduating—what do you mean?"

"You know, are you graduating or are you coming back next year?"

"Uh, I'm graduating, of course," I said, not wanting to ask her the same. I didn't really understand the question, though. I wasn't about to receive any summa cum laude honors for my performance or anything like that, but the truth is that, outside of the singular case of Playboy (who was deemed a failure and an unfortunate waste of talent), I had never asked or heard any of my non-black friends ask each other such a question as this, and the naturalness, the ingenuousness, with which she posed it astonished me, as if failing to earn a bachelor's degree within four years could be normal. Who was she hanging with? I wondered. It had been so long since I kept up with her and her friends. What were they thinking? How could that be OK? I thought about the fact that, for a long time, I had not been very welcome in her scene and I wasn't bitter, I appreciated that. I ordered myself a sandwich, forced a smile, and said good-bye.

When graduation day finally did come, Josh's family and mine had a dinner together, along with my maternal aunt and uncle, Sam and his mother and sister, and Betrys, who came down with my parents for the occasion. The dinner was long and happy and I have forgotten a lot of it, but I do have two loosely related memories from this night: The first and most vivid is the restrained pride that played across and lit up Pappy's face as he rose to his feet and toasted Josh and me, speaking off-the-cuff and employing rhetoric, beseeching us in English and then in Latin to go and seize the day, to venture into the world and to realize ourselves now as men, to remain on vigilant guard against the temptation to grow so narrowly ambitious that we forget the wisdom of Cicero and our duty to the good: *Non nobis solum nati sumus* ("We are not born for ourselves alone").

The other thing I remember from that night is the flickering, candlelit image of my uncle—a big, strong, good-hearted, God-fearing Southern white man—glimpsed through champagne-blurred eyes, taking me by the arm after coffee and dessert, guiding me to a corner of the room, and stating, man-to-man, that I was something like a fool if I did not marry the beautiful girl who had come down here with my parents for me.

I agreed with my uncle that he was right, I probably was a fool, but I could not marry that girl, not then. In a couple of months, I would be moving to the north of France, where I had accepted a yearlong post to teach English in secondary schools. Betrys hadn't tried to stop me from going, and I was as grateful to her for that as I was for all she had done over the years to help me recalibrate my thinking about both women and myself. She was in a period of transition now, too, scrapping plans to go to law school and enrolling in culinary school instead. I was proud of her for that, for having the courage to create her own path. I looked over my uncle's shoulder at her; she smiled at me, and right then everything felt good.

Though we were no longer as close as we had been, I was also extremely proud of Charles, who was graduating magna cum laude and at the top of his school's economics department. He would be starting as a trader at J. P. Morgan around the same time I would be leaving for Europe. We had developed very different ideas of what it means to make it in this world, Charles and I, and although I had myself lost the capacity to admire Wall Street, I also knew what he had overcome to get there, whom he had to muscle out of the way for the job. It was no small thing.

And when I reflected back on our post-prom trip to the Jersey Shore four years earlier, it occurred to me that some of the people who were there with us had since then gone to jail; some had sold and used drugs; most had drifted into lives of pure, unadulterated mediocrity; a few had babies they weren't prepared to raise; at least one had died. Charles and I were the only alumni from the group with our futures still intact, and that kind of bond doesn't easily unglue.

On one of the last evenings before I moved away, my friend Sam came to see me. Sam had decided a while ago that college wasn't for him and was working with his hands now. "The thing is, you just gotta know the consequences of your decisions," he said to me once. "I've accepted the fact that I'll be doing some form of manual labor for the rest of my life, backaches and all that shit. I don't have a problem with that, because I chose it. That's the difference between me and a lot of these knuckleheads out here, running around thinking Jermaine Dupri is gonna call 'em up with a record deal, or that fucking Pat Riley's got a spot for them on the team." Sam was a realist, and I always respected that about him.

That night, the two of us hopped into his old Cadillac Coupe de Ville and drove to the Kennedy Fried Chicken over in Plainfield. The last time I had been there was years ago with Stacey and, though I couldn't recall why now, I knew it had not been a good night. As I walked inside, it occurred to me that I didn't miss Stacey at all. When Sam and I had our food and got back into the car, he suggested we just ride around for a bit, for old times' sake. I said sure. Sam is a good driver to ride with, the kind of guy who is an expert on the area he grew up in, knows all the shortcuts and all the scenic routes. We drove all over Plainfield, zigzagging past Unisex Hair Creationz, past the few blocks of housing projects, and eventually past the park near Stacey's aunt's house where I had waited for my brother to come and get me. "Oh, I meant to tell you," he said, "I ran into Stacey at the grocery store the other day—she had *another* child, yo!"

"Oh, yeah?" I said, shaking my head.

"Yeah, she hadn't gained a pound, though, still looked pretty good."

"I'd expect that."

We looped back into Scotch Plains, down Front Street and past Antwan's mother's house. His car was parked outside. "And what about Ant, have you seen him lately?"

"Mmhmm. That nigga's a cashier up at Kohl's, still trying to get with every white girl he sees." We laughed. We passed RaShawn's family's house and neither of us had anything to say.

"And Larry?" I said, when we passed his.

"Still lives with his parents. He leased an Acura TL with a leather interior, put some nineteen-inch chrome rims on it, and now you can't tell him he's not on top of the world."

"Did he ever get a scholarship to play college ball?"

"I don't think so."

"He just hustles now?"

"I think so. Either that or he flips burgers at McDonald's and puts his entire paycheck on that car note."

We headed back toward my house, lapsing into a silence that lasted until we pulled up to my driveway. Sam put the car in park and turned to me. "You know what, man?" he said. "Like everybody else, I used to really think you were crazy, Thomas."

"Oh yeah?" I said, laughing.

"Hell yeah! All those times in the summer when it was nice as fuck out, and everyone was outside chilling, and you were just stuck inside studying. I used to feel bad for you and really wonder how you put up with that."

"I know. I used to wonder the same thing."

"Yeah, but all that studying paid off, man, and I'm proud of you."

I thanked Sam for his kind words. I wasn't sure when I'd see him again, so I told him that I loved him. It was past midnight now and as I walked up to my house, I could see through the picture window that Pappy's reading lamp was still lit. He was at his desk when I opened the door, underlining some pages in a book.

"You know, I just keep returning to Barzun, over and over again," he said, glancing up. He had taken an evening shower and looked fresh. "He really is a fine mind and you should read him." I pulled up a chair at the desk and we spoke for a moment about *From Dawn to Decadence*.

"Well, you'll be heading off soon, I guess," Pappy said, shifting gears.

"Yeah," I said, "it's getting close now." I didn't really know what to say. The truth is Pappy had not wanted me to go to France, and he had made that clear. His preference was for me to go straight through to graduate school and to get another degree before life had a chance to get in the way. I was defying him by going like this. But he had come to accept the fact that he taught me for years to think for myself and that this was the consequence. He had conceded the argument a long time ago.

"Well, let's play chess," he said, pounding the desk with his fist and smiling.

"Yeah, sure, Babe," I said, getting up to clear the desk for the board and looking at my father. Sometimes when he is sitting like this at his desk with a certain half-smile on his lips, and with his big, bald head and his hand balled tight into a fist, Pappy can look the way he does in certain pictures from his childhood. He looked that way to me right then, like a child. For a moment, I just watched him, and thoughts rushed through me. Just knowing where Pappy had come from, knowing from books and television a little bit about that period of the American century he had passed through with dark skin, standing there realizing that this man who looked like a child right then had never really gotten to be a child, had never had a father, I felt humbled and overwhelmed with pride in Pappy and I told him so.

"I'm so proud of you, Babe," I said, and he looked at me kind of surprised. He couldn't have known what was going through my mind, and my comment must have seemed to come from out of the blue.

"Oh, well, you just make sure you tell your grandkids about me. Tell 'em their great-grandpappy wasn't such a terrible man after all," he joked.

"Oh, I'll tell them about you!" I said. "I'll tell them you made me read books all day and play chess all night." We both laughed. I set down the board and asked Pappy which color he wanted, though I already knew the answer.

"Black, Thomas Chatterton," he said. "I've always wanted to be black."

Epilogue

I

Yo soy yo y mi circunstancia ("I am myself and my circumstance"), José Ortega y Gasset wrote before being forced to flee Franco's Spain and enter into years of exile in Argentina. I encountered this deceptively simple sentence while living and working in France. It was a time, just after graduating college, when my own circumstances were diverging drastically from those I had known as a child growing up in New Jersey—a time when I was thinking seriously about that fact, about who I was and where I was headed. Those little epiphanies I had imagined and wished for while reading Shelby Steele's *Harper's* essay had begun to hit me and, like Eddie, I was understanding on an almost physical level that awesome boundlessness a black American can feel outside of America. I was also realizing that we simply do not often see ourselves very accurately on our own and it is only through other people that we glimpse or comprehend our own situations or selves. These others sometimes come to us in the form of wise authors and compelling characters (real or fictitious), and sometimes as ordinary people whom we meet and know in everyday life. When we are lucky, these different sources of revelation converge into one stream of truth and we really do see ourselves, as we are or have been. This convergence happened in a notable way for me on two separate occasions in France.

On the first, which took place soon after my arrival, as often happens in a foreign country I found myself hanging out at a perfect stranger's home. He was a literature student named Stéphane, with whom I had some friends in common. A couple of us ended up at his place one night after dinner. "What would you like to drink?" Stéphane asked me, playing some music on his CD player.

"What do you have?" I said.

"There is some beer, a little red wine, and I have a bit of Armagnac, as well." Louis Armstrong's trumpet and raspy voice belted from the speakers, flooding the room with New Orleans.

"Armagnac, please," I said, and he returned with a bottle and several glasses. We sipped the brandy slowly, enjoying the jazz. Everyone in the room—all Franco-French white kids, it occurred to me—knew their Louis Armstrong inside and out, knew the names of the songs, had their favorites. That is phenomenal, I thought.

"How do you guys know so much about black music?" I asked.

"Are you kidding?" Stéphane, replied, assuming, I think, that I was implying only an American could be so well versed. "This is something the whole world knows. Practically everything except classical is black music!" I refilled my glass with the brandy, which, I noticed, tasted an awful lot like Hennessy—better, though.

It's strange, I began to think, None of the black kids I grew up with would have said something like that. "Practically everything except classical is black music." I thought of the way we all referred to house music as white, or of the way no one even knew George Clinton and Parliament Funkadelic were largely from Plainfield. It was a restricted way of understanding things—kind of like the way no one ever drank brandy that wasn't Hennessy. I explained to Stéphane that he had got me wrong: I was giving him props—it was not true that the whole world knew these things.

The second time such a convergence happened was near the end of my stay. My friends Shadik and Shadir, along with Josh, had come to visit, and I took them to Paris for the weekend. The twins had never left the country before and they were as awestruck as I had been when I first saw another part of the world. After a day spent crisscrossing the Seine, strolling Saint-Germain, staring at the Louvre—"That's where the kings used to live, right?"—sitting in the gardens, darting in and out of the bookstores, clothing stores, and pastry shops, the four of us decided to end the evening on the rue Saint-Honoré with a bottle of wine at Hôtel Costes.

We went inside and got a table in one of the back rooms next to what Josh thought was a well-known Brazilian Formula One race-car driver and across from a big party of celebrating Arabs. A statuesque black waitress, who looked a lot like Grace Jones but with long, straightened hair, brought a bottle of Bordeaux and some square plates of olives for us to pick at. Bossa nova and electronic tango music complemented the surroundings the way the cerigno-las did the wine. All day the twins had been soaking up the city, wowed repeatedly by its splendor and grace. Now they were visibly tired. We sank into our seats and talked, with the certainty of young people who are just learning something, about the importance of getting out and seeing things. Everyone was in agreement about this. But the more we talked and the more the room filled with some rather entitled-looking people who appeared as if they had seen plenty of the world themselves, the more the strange and foreign sounds mixed with the strange and unfamiliar tastes, I noticed that the expressions on the twins' faces were changing, gradually, almost imperceptibly at first, from awe to uncertainty. "What is this music?" Shadir asked me. "Why have I never heard anything like this before?" We laughed, but he was serious.

"I've never even seen olives like these," said Shadik. "Are they good?"

"Do you sometimes feel uncomfortable in spots like this?" Shadir asked, the questions coming one after the other.

"I never even knew spots like this existed," Shadik said, staring at his drink.

After the initial everything-is-wonderful shock of the new had worn off, and wholly outside the range of their traditional points of reference, I could see that the twins were now beginning to feel like they were losing their footing. I knew exactly what that felt like, what they were going through right then. It wasn't that they had come to Paris and developed an inferiority complex, concluding— voilà!—that what they really wanted was to be French, to be white; that that would somehow be better. It wasn't anything close to that. In my experience, black people don't often actually want to be white.

No, I knew what they were feeling right then, and it was something else. If you're young and black today and lucky enough to get out and travel, see the world beyond your own little backyard, inevitably it is going to strike you that you have been lied to. You have been straight-up lied to, and not just in the most obvious way—not just by Robert L. Johnson and the propaganda organ of BET or by the spokesmen for stereotypes, the Busta Rhymeses and the Gucci Manes. It's worse than that; the swindling has gone down far closer to home. You have been lied to by people you have known personally, people you have trusted, your friends and your neighbors, your older siblings and your classmates, your cousins and your lovers. Whether that lie is born of simple ignorance masquerading as arrogance—a seductive ignorance, yes, but still only ignorance—or, worse, actual malice, matters little at the moment of your realization. All that matters at that moment is the lie itself, this fiction that says that for you and your kind alone an authentic existence is a severely limited one. You have been lied to (and for how long?) and now you know that you have been lied to and you can't deny it and you are naked.

The twins, under the influence of a day of discovery and not a little wine, were going through this revelation in front of me, I could see it in their faces, their searching, contemplating faces, and I knew it at first glance because I had gone through it too, many times before. At last, they could see the lie, which they had never previously glimpsed; it was right there in the room with them, tethered over the table like a fluorescent helium balloon, and no more impenetrable than that—they could reach out and touch it, puncture it with a fork or a toothpick if they wanted. And that hurts.

Sitting there at Hôtel Costes or in the Jardin du Luxembourg or in the Tuileries or just at some humble neighborhood brasserie, where finally it occurs to you that a bloody piece of meat actually tastes good, or at Dean & Deluca, where you encounter your first baguette, you think to yourself: I kind of like this. "This" being cheese, or wine, or bread, or fresh spinach leaves. Or crossing your legs, or polite conversation, or Renaissance art, or serious books. Or music that is not rap, or curiosity, or cosmopolitanism—in short, education, edification, exposure, whatever you want to call it. That is, whatever it is you used to think wasn't real, wasn't strictly for the N.I.G.G.A.s. You think to yourself: If only someone had told me all this was out here, I might have paid better attention in school! You think to yourself: This isn't fair. It gets you hot and vexed.

And then, all of a sudden, when you feel as if you can't take it anymore, when you think there must be some exculpating explanation, some scenario that will allow you to pass the blame—it must be because you're black and these things aren't intended for people like you in the first place, that racism is what it's really all about—some Malian or Sudanese (yes, Sudanese!) chick walks by, all ebony-complected, all elegant and arresting, fluent in French and English as well as some obscure tribal dialect, and you realize this isn't a skin thing, a color thing, a hair-texture thing, or even a money thing anymore (your childhood was comfortable enough). No, this is a culture thing, and yours has limited and cheated you profoundly. And then the final realization: You have been lying to yourself all this time—The Supreme Lie—you have been an accomplice, a co-architect of your own ignorance. And that really hurts, because you're not a dummy. I knew what they were feeling because I had felt it many times before. In the twins I could see myself, and long after they had left, I reflected on the stifling circumstances in which we'd all grown up.

II

And yet, as I sit here now, recounting those two nights several years ago—nights that really started this book for me—I am filled mostly with hope, not pessimism. Has there ever been a more exciting time than the present to be young and black in America? Overnight, it seems as though the vistas of circumstance have opened up for us dramatically: Suddenly, the most powerful man in the country is not white, he is black; and the most visible black person in the world is not a thug or entertainer, he is a nuanced thinker. I have asked my father many times how such a development makes him feel. "Son, you are living in a different world," he says. "This is no longer my world. The question is: How does this make *you* feel?"

The more pressing question, though, is, How will this make subsequent generations of black people feel? Will such a twist in the American racial narrative prove powerful enough to alter the underlying laws that still govern day-to-day black life? Will we, at long last, allow ourselves to abandon the instinct to self-sabotage and the narcissistic glorification of our own failure? Will the fact of daily exposure to a black president in turn expose once and for all the lie that is and always has been *keeping it real*?

Since the dawn of the hip-hop era in the 1970s, black people have become increasingly freer and freer as individuals, with a wider range of possibilities spread out before us now than at any time in our past. Yet the circumstances of our collective life have degenerated in direct contrast to this fact, with a more impoverished vision of what it means to be black today than ever before. If these exciting new circumstances we now find ourselves in, of which our black president is the apotheosis, are to mean anything of lasting value, the zeitgeist (Hegel), the They (Heidegger), or whatever we might call it, *this* is going to have to change, too—and permanently.

It is more accurate to say, however, that the mood of black culture doesn't need to *change* into something wholly new so much as it must simply find a way to *reclaim* what it once had. One of the most fascinating paradoxes the student of black history ever observes, as well as a tremendous justification for black pride, is the extent to which this culture, against all likelihood, has customarily embodied a joyful, soulful, affirming approach to life and not a spiritually bankrupt or self-defeating one. It is only very recently—basically within my brother's lifetime, which is to say, the three and a half decades of the hip-hop era or, roughly, the post–Civil Rights era—that this has, in the main, ceased to be the case. In other words, it is only *after* the tremendous civil-rights victories of the '60s, only after desegregation, only after affirmative action that black America has become so militantly provincial and wildly nihilistic.

Why has such undeniable societal progress been met with such obvious cultural regress? Why when external limitations have been—and still are being—lifted do we frantically search for replacement constraints to bring down on ourselves? Is this, ultimately, what slavery's residue tastes like? Is this the legacy of Jim

Crow? Or is it, as some do argue, that the black community simply fell apart with integration? Is white flight to blame here? Was it crack? Was it AIDS? Is there an inherent bias in the nation's criminal justice system? Is it all of the above, just some toxic mix, or something else entirely? I am not a sociologist and do not presume to have a catchall theory; I only know what I have seen. Perhaps it is the case, as many have claimed, that hip-hop culture is nothing but the logical outcome of the profound and alienating experiences so many blacks have had in the great American cities in the decades following the Civil Rights movement. Perhaps it is simply the result of all that disillusionment all those blacks and their children surely must have felt. Perhaps this is true. Be that as it may, though, are we bound now to keep the alienation and disillusionment going; are we bound to keep this culture that was born in negativity running in perpetuity?

In college it tripped me out to think that Hegel could have understood the slave and not the master as the ascendant consciousness. Unlikely as it may seem, though, many blacks in the past have seen things this way, too. There is a joy, an aliveness— after all, it is the slave, Hegel wrote, who *loves* life—a spirit that has manifested itself throughout the course of African-American history. It is a way of working hard and taking pride in one's work, of laughing through tears and coping with miserable circumstances. It is a way of transforming blind hatred into beautiful music, bad cuts of meat into delicious meals. It is a way of turning searing pain into quiet strength. It is what Ralph Ellison called *discipline*—a quality he saw as inherent in black culture and something he believed, ultimately, would prove to be the salve to heal the racial sickness that plagued the country in which he lived. Ellison's idea

of discipline, of course, has roots in W.E.B. Du Bois and his conception of the new Negro youth:

> We black folk may help [mankind] for we have within us as a
> race new stirrings; stirrings of the beginning of a new
> appreciation of joy, of a new desire to create, of a new will to
> be ... and there has come the conviction that the youth that is
> here today, the Negro youth, is a different kind of youth ... with a
> new realization of itself, with new determination for all mankind.

How poignantly do these words capture what was to come—
the figure of Martin Luther King, the jazz of John Coltrane, the
fiction of Ralph Ellison, the nonviolent Civil Rights movement of
the 1960s? How ludicrous and naïve, how wildly off base, do they
seem now in the age of 50 Cent? The above quote is from a 1926
speech entitled "The Criteria of Negro Art," which Du Bois delivered in Chicago to a gathering of descendants of slaves. A deep
reader of philosophy himself, he would have been aware of the
Hegelian notes ringing through him. Consider what else Du Bois
had to say:

> If you tonight suddenly should become full-fledged Americans; if
> your color faded, or the color line here in Chicago was
> miraculously forgotten; suppose, too, you became at the same
> time rich and powerful;—what is it that you would want? What
> would you immediately seek? Would you buy the most powerful
> of motor cars and outrace Cook County? Would you buy the most
> elaborate estate on the North Shore? Would you be a Rotarian or
> a Lion or a What-not of the very last degree? Would you wear the

most striking clothes, give the richest dinners, and buy the
longest press notices?

Even as you visualize such ideals you know in your hearts that
these are not the things you really want. You realize this sooner
than the average white American because, pushed aside as we
have been in America, there has come to us not only a certain
distaste for the tawdry and flamboyant but a vision of what the
world could be if it were really a beautiful world; if we had
the true spirit; if we had the Seeing Eye, the Cunning Hand, the
Feeling Heart; if we had, to be sure, not perfect happiness, but
plenty of good hard work, the inevitable suffering that always
comes with life; sacrifice and waiting, all that—but, nevertheless,
lived in a world where men know, where men create, where they
realize themselves and where they enjoy life. It is that sort of a
world we want to create for ourselves and for all America.

The man raises some questions that are worthy of reconsidera-
tion: If blacks were to become rich and powerful, just what, exactly, would we want from life? Would that something be *more*
than "the most powerful of motor cars"? "Pushed aside as we have
been," would we exhibit a "distaste for the tawdry and flamboyant"? Would we seek to create a new sort of world, a world where
men *realize themselves*?

Some of the finest minds of the nineteenth and twentieth centuries contemplated these same questions and could not imagine
that the slave consciousness—that modest vessel for the progression
of human spirit—would evolve into the petty, limited, money-hoes-
and-clothes-obsessed consciousness of today, that Malcolm X's "By

any means necessary" cry for dignity and freedom would, in just three decades' time, get butchered into Kanye West's soulless "Buy any jeans necessary" claptrap. That black life in America has suffered a tremendous loss of *discipline* and *spirit* in the hip-hop era is a fact meticulously documented throughout the culture.

III

Nietzsche believed the greatest deeds are thoughts. "The world revolves around the inventors of new values," he wrote. For more than thirty years the black world has revolved around the inventors of hip-hop values, and this has been a decisive step backward. My generation, if we are to make it and to make good on the debt we owe our ancestors, must find a new vocabulary and another point of view. We have to reclaim the discipline and the spirit we have lost. We have to flip the script on what it means to be black. We have to think about what is and is not beneficial to our own mental, cultural, and even physical health. As a people, we have emerged from centuries spent in the dark woods of slavery and racism only to come upon an ominous forking path. It is hardly an exaggeration to say that our survival will be determined by the direction that we take. If we can't change our ideas, if we fail to cultivate future generations of personalities that are something more than just cool—or hard—if we fail to realize that certain values are better, and worse, than others, then what we are doing is presiding over our own gradual destruction. And that is something, for my father's generation, that not even the most fanatic Klansmen could have hoped to achieve.

"Suppose the only Negro who survived some centuries hence was the Negro painted by white Americans in the novels and essays they have written. What would people in a hundred years say of black Americans?" Du Bois asked that gathering of descendants of slaves. This was a serious concern for forward-looking blacks in the 1920s, but today it feels anachronistic. Just imagine, however, if the only black American who survived one hundred years from now was that cartoonish thug of the past thirty years, so vividly wrought on the canvas of hip-hop music and culture. Would that not be equally depressing? Would that not be *worse* since, after all, we have drawn this grotesque with our own hand?

IV

On the day before the MTV Video Music Awards this past September, I found myself walking on the Lower East Side of New York City. Manhattan, the downtown portion of it at least, was overflowing with the kind of moneyed young blacks the rap industry has produced in startlingly large numbers over recent years. I was walking along Rivington Street with an attractive girl and we were approaching a tall, thirtyish black guy who was dressed from head to toe in brands you would find at Bergdorf Goodman and Barneys. He was struggling with several bulging shopping bags from Louis Vuitton, and as we passed he noticed us and turned, peering over his Tom Ford frames to say to my date, "I just throw it in the bag; I just throw it in the bag!" He was referencing one of the most popular and ubiquitous rap songs of the moment, Fabolous's vapid ode to shopping without looking at price tags, which was surprising, since he did not, on first glance, appear to be confined by the categories and thought processes of hip-hop at all. He had on the kind of tight-fitting, ultra-expensive European threads Playboy wore in college, gear that has as much to do with keeping it real and 'hood living as Sub-Zero kitchen appliances do. What was so striking to me about this man the more I thought about him—even more than his lovely and costly garments—was the fact that wealthy and seemingly worldly as he may have been, as flush with resources and credit as he may have been, he was actually *living* the inane lyrics of a rap song as unthinkingly and literal-mindedly as the most hard-core and insulated thug.

Of course, I immediately recognized the song he was quoting because I also listen to the music. I don't think it's possible to shut your eyes and ears completely to a culture as pervasive and aesthetically seductive as hip-hop—and I wonder whether it would even be desirable to do that. I don't fault this man for being aware of what is simply around him. I do, though, find myself contemplating and feeling sorry for the guy. It is precisely this intangible smallness of mind and inability to transcend skin-deep superficiality, this moral childishness and sheepish conformity, that is the root problem in black life today and the true subject of this book.

The fact is that this problem can never be solved simply by smashing up all the Snoop Dogg albums, as the Reverend Calvin Butts has tried to do, or by banning the most offensive hip-hop fashions, as the city of Baltimore once considered. The better approach—if the far more difficult one—would be for us to learn, once and for all, how to interpret and navigate the world around us, and to stop confusing the shoes on our feet or the songs in our ears for ourselves.

ACKNOWLEDGMENTS

A book does not belong to its author alone—many people give shape to it. Which is not to imply that anyone listed below necessarily shares any of the views advanced in this work. Rather, it is simply to say that without these people's presence, the book and I would have been far poorer.

I want to express my deepest thanks to my parents, who have worked so hard and of whom I am so proud. Both of you inspire me to want to be better than I am.

Truman Capote wrote, "Anyone who ever gave you confidence, you owe them a lot." I am indebted to my teacher, mentor, and friend Katie Roiphe more than I could ever possibly say or repay. In those fragile early phases of writing when a little class assignment attempts to become an op-ed, which then somehow attempts to become a viable book proposal, it was Katie who gave me the confidence to believe my goals were not beyond my reach. In addition to being brilliant, she was kind and tremendously generous with me. I cannot imagine this book existing without the insight, guidance, reassurance, and encouragement she provided along the way.

I need to thank my agent, Elyse Cheney, for taking a chance on me, for refusing to send out my proposal until it was ready, and when it finally was, for schlepping all over New York City with me in the rain while fighting off a wicked cold. I could not have asked for a better person to work with. Many thanks to Nicole Steen and Hannah Elnan at Cheney Literary Associates.

Toni Morrison once said that editors "are like priests or psychiatrists, the wrong one can do more harm than good, but the right one is worth searching for." I consider myself very lucky to have found mine. Eamon Dolan is not only a diplomat and a gentleman, but something like a cross between a Neapolitan tailor and a gadfly, trimming and trimming, prodding and prodding, until somewhere along the line a bloated and unruly Microsoft Word document comes to resemble a finished work. Thanks also to Nicole Hughes and everyone else at Penguin who worked so hard on this project.

I am indebted to my big brother, Clarence, who bought me my first laptop and who opened his home to me when I badly needed a room of my own in which to write. I'm proud of you, Clarence. On the topic of rooms, I need to give special thanks to my brothers-from-other-mothers, Carlos Larkin, Joshua Yaffa, and Shahin Vallée, each of whom at various stages of the writing process kept me company, lodged me, and sometimes even fed me in London, Boston, Brooklyn, and Paris. All of you I need to thank for your candid feedback, encouragement, and critical engagement with this book. Josh, especially, I need to thank you for the constant use of your ears, eyes, and apartment; Shahin, for personally making my dream of living and writing in Paris come alive; and Carlos, for all those things that had the two of us in tears that night at the bar in TriBeCa, and much more besides that. Godspeed, brothers.

This book may never have got off the ground without the extraordinary help on so many levels that I received from Berthsy Ayide. Thank you so much for everything.

Many thanks to David Howell, Katherine Howell, and Karen Moore, my second family, for their love and support. Many thanks to Charone and Chamir Shivers, my little brothers, for their belief in me.

I want to thank Noah Eaker for his early encouragement and very helpful feedback, as well as Ashley and John Paul Lech in New York and the Roussell family in Los Angeles for their supreme hospitality.

I am grateful to the faculty at the Cultural Reporting and Criticism program at NYU, specifically the late Ellen Willis and the current director, Susie Linfield, for the generous fellowship they awarded me, which made graduate school a possibility; and to the distinguished writer in residence Paul Berman for the hours of stimulating conversation he gave me free of charge. I also want to thank my CRC classmates for creating a thought-provoking and lively atmosphere in which to fall in love with words and writing.

Finally, I have to recognize three very special professors from Georgetown, Marcia Morris, Patrick Laude, and Wilfried Ver Eecke, each of whom taught me at crucial junctures how to think and that I could think. Thank you.